The EHCP Handbook

How to Make an Effective Education Health and Care Plan

A guide for parents and carers

Ekaterina Harrison

SOS SEN

Pavilion
PUBLISHING

The EHCP Handbook

© Pavilion Publishing & Media

The author has asserted her rights in accordance with the Copyright, Designs and Patents Act (1988) to be identified as the author of this work.

Published by:

Pavilion Publishing and Media Ltd
Blue Sky Offices
25 Cecil Pashley Way
Shoreham by Sea
West Sussex
BN43 5FF

Tel: +44(0)1273 434 943
Email: info@pavpub.com
Web: www.pavpub.com

Published 2024

A catalogue record for this book is available from the British Library.

ISBN: 978-1-803883-95-3

Pavilion Publishing and Media is a leading publisher of books, training materials and digital content in mental health, social care and allied fields. Pavilion and its imprints offer must-have knowledge and innovative learning solutions underpinned by sound research and professional values.

Author: Ekaterina Harrison
Editor: Vivenne Button
Cover design: Emma Dawe, Pavilion Publishing and Media Ltd
Page layout and typesetting: Phil Morash, Pavilion Publishing and Media Ltd
Illustrations: © James Harrison 2024
Printing: Halstan & Co Ltd

This book is dedicated to all neurodivergent children and young people who struggle at school.

On the following page, you will see the artwork created by my son. He drew a variety of school bags, each belonging to a different child. Just as these bags are diverse, so are the learners they represent. Within this varied group, some of them may be autistic or have conditions such as attention deficit hyperactivity disorder (ADHD), dyslexia, or others. Much like the items concealed within each bag, these disabilities may not be immediately visible. To describe these learners the term 'neurodivergent' is used, which refers to someone whose brain operates in ways that differ from what is typically seen as the norm. These differences can significantly influence these children's and young people's needs and how they learn.

More and more cases are emerging of neurodivergent children who face challenges in accessing the education they need. Several factors contribute to this trend, including growing numbers of diagnoses, increased awareness of underlying issues, and difficulties within traditional educational settings. While laws and policies are evolving to promote inclusivity in education, there are transitional challenges. Persistent budgetary constraints add an extra layer of complexity to an already difficult situation.

According to the school census in 2023, autism is the most common type of condition among those with an Education, Health and Care Plan (EHCP) in England. Although this book was written with all special educational needs in mind, it is acknowledged that many readers will be turning to it for advice on supporting neurodivergent children and young people.

As a society, we really must make sure that all these kids have the chance to learn in a way that works for them. Every child deserves a chance to reach their full potential.

About the author

Ekaterina Harrison is a solicitor qualified to practise law in England and Wales. Originally from Russia, she settled in the UK many years ago and lives in London with her family. As an autistic woman and a mother to three neurodivergent children, she brings a unique perspective to her writing on special needs and legal entitlements. Her expertise in education law has developed through advocacy work for her children's needs and volunteering with the charity SOS!SEN.

The illustrations inside the book are by the author's son, James (age 11). His work was exhibited at the Royal Academy Young Artists' Summer Show in 2023.

Acknowledgements

I am deeply grateful for all support and encouragement I received from my family throughout the journey of writing this book. Your presence was my guiding light and I could not have completed this endeavour without you by my side. My special thanks go to my talented son James for bringing the pages of this book to life with his extraordinary illustrations.

I also want to express my thanks to everyone who took the time to read my draft book, share feedback and provide comments. My sincere appreciation goes to Lauren Jurgensen, Dr Gillian Pyke, Marion Strudwick, Dr Elisabeth, Julia Katulevska, Kat Eremina, Hilary Malcolm and Wessie du Toit for their invaluable assistance and advice. A special acknowledgement is owed to Elizaveta Kharchenko for her assistance with digitising my son's illustrations. Thank you all so much.

I would like to express my immense gratitude to everyone at Barnes Primary School, the most incredible primary school this side of the Milky Way. With your support, I have gained invaluable insights into how dedicated educators can uplift their students to unimaginable heights. Together, we have been on a journey of discovery, expanding our knowledge and overcoming challenges as a team.

Furthermore, I want to acknowledge the powerful influence of my time volunteering with the charity SOS!SEN. The dedication and compassion I witnessed there served as inspiration for this book. These pages stand as a tribute to the incredible impact that this organisation and its volunteers have on so many families with children and young people who have SEN and disabilities.

Moreover, I extend my heartfelt thanks to the law firm I have been working at, Katten, for its resolute dedication to pro bono work. I sincerely appreciate the chances you have given me to contribute to causes that are personally significant and truly meaningful. I express deep gratitude to my colleagues, Christopher Hitchins and Charlotte Sallabank, for providing my book with unwavering support in every possible way.

Table of Contents

Tables

Preface

Imagine stepping into a bright and cosy classroom where an enthusiastic teacher stands at the front, ready with a whiteboard marker and imaginative handouts. The teacher's eyes shine with a strong desire to ignite a spark in every child's heart. The room buzzes with anticipation as both eager and hesitant learners await the day's lesson.

Yet some of the children within this idyllic scene face extraordinary challenges on their learning journey. Their path is strewn with obstacles that, to them, may feel insurmountable, causing them to struggle in ways that their peers may not understand. For these brave souls, the traditional education environment is a daily battlefield, in which every step forward is an uphill climb.

I have first-hand experience of challenges like these, because my three children have faced similar barriers. To ensure they had access to education, we as a family had to stand and fight tough battles, find our way through complex and challenging processes, and advocate relentlessly for their rights every inch of the way.

Within our familial circle, we are acutely aware of the challenges faced by neurodivergent children. Terms such as autism, ADHD, Pathological Demand Avoidance (PDA), Auditory Processing Disorder (APD), Sensory Processing Disorder (SPD) or Avoidant Restrictive Food Intake Disorder (ARFID) are not some foreign or mysterious codes to us. Since the early years of my children's lives, we have dealt with speech delays, communication issues and sensory difficulties. We are familiar with prosopagnosia (face recognition blindness) and know how to manage alexithymia (emotional blindness). This has been and continues to be a difficult path to navigate.

My background as a lawyer proved indispensable in this journey. It enabled me to evaluate critically the framework that is used to assess and meet children's needs from both a personal and professional perspective. This combination of skills and experience helped me to gain valuable knowledge that I am eager to share, so that others may benefit from the lessons we learned. This was my motivation behind writing this guide.

While the primary audience for this book is families, I believe it will also be of interest to professionals who work in the field of special needs. Local authority (LA) officers may gain knowledge from the examples shared, and school Special Educational Needs Co-ordinators (SENCOs) may find it a useful reference tool. Teachers might be interested to learn more about how things work.

I sincerely hope that this book proves to be a valuable resource for everyone who reads it.

Foreword

Eleanor Wright
Legal Officer, SOS!SEN

Over the course of several years working with the parents and carers of children and young people with special educational needs and disabilities, particularly in relation to securing and enforcing the children's legal rights in education, I have become only too well aware of the minefield this area of the law can seem to present.

Parents of children with SEND, who of course already have their hands extremely full in dealing with all that is involved with supporting their children, suddenly find themselves having to negotiate processes which can seem complex and arcane simply to secure the help their children desperately need. Although there is theoretically a network of support in place to help them, accessing it is not easy, and it is made more complex because of gatekeeping practices designed to save money by cutting down the number of families receiving support to which they are entitled by law. Parents find themselves trusting local authority and education professionals to advise them as to what their child is entitled to, only to discover far too often that what they are told is simply wrong – sometimes as a result of deliberate misrepresentation, but all too frequently because the professionals concerned are themselves misinformed, inadequately trained, and struggling with impossible caseloads. Ironically, the avalanche of information available online does not necessarily help, because it can be hard to pick out what is reliable from some sources that are frighteningly inaccurate.

One of our aims at SOS!SEN is to redress this by offering easy access to help and information through a variety of means, and also by offering advice directly to parents and carers through our helpline, drop-in advice centres and other services. We therefore meet a very wide range of parents and hear about a very wide spectrum of problems, and even after well over two decades in this field I can still be surprised by the sheer variety and inventiveness of the ways in which public authorities can get the law wrong and seek to evade their statutory duties. Over the years, I have often said that if we had a motto, it would be along the lines that "Knowledge is power", and it is that power that we aim to give parents. In this field, the parent/carer who knows the law and can use both the law and the relevant appeal and enforcement procedures effectively is automatically in a very strong position. Generally, they will find that this places them in by far the best position for constructive and productive dealings with their local authorities and children's schools or other placements to secure the best outcomes. However, we are always all too well aware that we can only help a limited number of parents and children, and that there are far too many cases where children do not receive their legal entitlement because their families, through no fault of their own, do not know what that entitlement is nor how to secure it.

I therefore really welcome the publication of *The EHCP Handbook* as an up-to-date and very accessible source of information on one of the most important aspects of the process affecting how children receive essential support in education. As a charity reliant on volunteers. the majority of whom are parents of children with SEND, we are well aware of the value to other parents of talking to people who have direct personal experience of the SEND system and how it works. That is one of the fundamental aspects of the value of this book: the author's direct experience of going through the SEND system with her children gives a perspective which cannot be duplicated through legal training. It is all too frequently the case that navigating through the SEND system is a matter of strategy and psychology as much as it is a matter of knowing the law. This is a very valuable tool for the families of children and young people with SEND in securing the power that knowledge gives.

What this book is – and is not – about

The area of special educational needs, or SEN, is a vast and diverse domain that covers a wide range of topics and concerns.

A family's first introduction to SEN typically occurs when it becomes apparent that a child needs assistance to thrive academically. This could be because they struggle to learn at the same pace as their peers. It could also be because the child has a disability that prevents them from using the facilities offered in mainstream schools or other educational settings.

For children who are not yet in school, there may be early recognition that – without support – accessing mainstream education will be challenging for them. In many cases, parents become concerned after their child has received a diagnosis of autism or conditions such as ADHD or dyslexia.

Once someone has identified the need for additional support, the next step is to start a process with the LA that is called an Education, Health and Care (EHC) needs assessment. The application can be made by parents, young people, schools or other placements.

To initiate the EHC needs assessment, specific criteria must be met. If the LA agrees that an assessment is warranted, experts are contacted and asked to provide detailed advice on the child's or young person's education requirements. Based on this assessment, if it is deemed necessary to provide special educational provision (SEP), the LA will issue an EHCP.

This book focuses specifically on the content of an EHCP, and how to get it right.

It should be borne in mind that the parents and young people do not write the EHCP, with the exception of Section A. The LA has an overall responsibility for drafting and revising the plan, yet families have a right to provide input and express their perspectives on its content.

Understanding what information is required in each section – as well as why that information is needed – will go a long way in advocating for what the child or young person needs, ensuring better outcomes.

There is a common misconception that obtaining an EHCP guarantees smooth sailing thereafter. It is important to realise that if the plan is not well written, it can end up being an empty document. Worse, it can create a false sense of accomplishment for the LA and educators and lead to the provision of support that ultimately misses the mark.

Imagine a poorly drafted EHCP as a chocolate teapot. It may look appealing and have fancy words written all over it but, when put to use, it quickly melts away without providing any valuable assistance. It also leaves a great big mess for someone to clean up and may damage the things with which it was intended to be used.

The plan, like a teapot, needs to be fit for purpose. You – whether you are a parent, teacher, or fill any other role – should not be left to handle both the clean-up and the search for the right teapot for the job. That is why it is vital to ensure that the EHCP is carefully written to provide clear guidance and support for the child's or young person's education journey.

Within these pages, you will find a careful examination of each section of the EHCP. The book addresses some common practices involved in writing them. It analyses the language that EHCPs use and shows you how to gain the necessary skills to write a plan that is accurate and specific.

This book also covers why EHCPs are significant, their historical context, and the key laws and regulations that govern this field. In addition, strategies are explored that can help families to maintain the plan's relevance and keep it up to date. The book also has sections on the identification of SEN and advocacy.

There are many other important subjects within the field of SEN. Appeals to the SEN and Disability Tribunal, mediations, dealing with school exclusions, transport issues, disability discrimination, and similar topics all deserve comprehensive coverage that should include practical publications and drafting guides.

Although this book does not address these matters, their significance and the need for further study cannot be understated. For those interested in this field, further research in these areas can be very rewarding.

Important points before we get started

The law and legal practices

Before we dive into the subject of this book, it is best to lay down some rules.

In terms of its geographical scope, the book is aimed to provide you with a general understanding of the law and legal practices in England. Wales, Scotland and Northern Ireland have their own distinctive regulations and systems in the area of SEN, but they are not covered within these pages.

The goal is to explore the topic of SEN and how individual EHCPs can support a child's or young person's needs. Think of this book as your guiding torchlight: it illuminates the legal landscape and directs you on your journey to find where you need to go. However, even though it is packed with valuable insights, it cannot replace specific professional legal advice from a qualified lawyer or other legal practitioner.

It is important to remember that the book's content is not tailored to your specific circumstances and it does not cover every tiny detail or unravel all the complexities of particular legal issues.

So, please do not delay seeking legal advice and do not disregard professional recommendations or make legal decisions based solely on what you read here. Legal matters require careful consideration and personalised, professional guidance to achieve the best results.

Lastly, bear in mind that laws and regulations may change over time. To stay up to date and ensure that you have the most accurate information, consult updated sources or seek expert guidance. Refer to the "online resources" section at the end of this book for a list of materials that can help you to stay on top of things.

Use of examples

This book shares many examples of how different sections of the EHCP can be written. The goal is to make the content relatable and easy to understand. I hope you will find these examples helpful.

Unless it is specifically mentioned that the example wording is sourced directly from a court case, the suggested phraseology is fictional and is intended purely for illustrative purposes. Any resemblances or coincidences between the example wording and real-life individuals or situations are unintentional.

Glossary

This book uses many legal terms and abbreviations that may be new to readers. Bookmark and use this glossary to help you keep track of them. If you need to look something up, you can always flip back to this page.

CFA 2014 The Children and Families Act 2014.

Child (children) A person or people who is/are not older than compulsory school age, as defined in Section 579 of the EA 1996.

Compulsory school age As defined in Section 8 of the EA 1996, a child is considered of compulsory school age from the first day of the term that starts after they turn five (or on their birthday if it falls on the first day of term) until the school leaving date – presently defined as the last Friday in June of the academic year in which they turn 16.

CSDPA 1970 The Chronically Sick and Disabled Persons Act 1970.

EA 1996 The Education Act 1996, which was the key Act in the context of SEN prior to the enactment of the CFA 2014. Some provisions are still in effect.

EHC needs assessment An assessment of the education, health and social care needs of a child or young person, as defined in Section 36(2) of the CFA 2014. It is commonly abbreviated as EHCNA.

EHCP An Education, Health and Care Plan, as defined in Section 37 of the CFA 2014.

EOTAS "Education otherwise than at a setting" – this term is used in Section 61 of the CFA 2014 to outline the right to receive EOTAS when a traditional school setting is deemed inappropriate.

EqA 2010   The Equality Act 2010 provides a legal framework in the context of children and young people with disabilities.

FTT   The First-Tier Tribunal is an independent court-like body at which parents (on behalf of a child) or young people (on their own account) can appeal decisions related to the EHCP process and EHCPs. It is also known as the "SEND Tribunal", "SENDIST" or "tribunal".

IPSEA   Independent Provider of Special Education Advice – a prominent charity that offers free legal advice, resources, and support to parents and carers of children with SEN and disabilities.

LA   The relevant Local Authority responsible for education provision, as set out in Section 24 of the CFA 2014.

NHS   The National Health Service is the publicly funded healthcare system in the United Kingdom.

Parent(s)   Birth parents or any individual who – despite not being a birth parent – either holds parental responsibility for a child or young person or is responsible for their care, as defined in Section 576 of the EA 1996.

Personal budget Funds earmarked by the LA for EHCP provision. These can be allocated directly to parents or young people to enable them to arrange the necessary support independently, rather than relying on the LA for co-ordination.

SEN   Special Educational Needs, in the form that this term is defined in Section 20 of the CFA 2014. The term covers a child's or young person's learning difficulties and disabilities that mean they need extra help in the form of SEP. Not all disabilities require this extra support; to cover those, this book occasionally mentions both SEN and disabilities separately, depending on context.

SENCO Special Educational Needs Co-ordinator – a designated individual tasked with overseeing SEN provision within a school.

SEN statement The document from the EA 1996. It is now a piece of history, served as the predecessor to what is currently known as an EHCP.

SEN support The assistance and support provided to a child or young person, as outlined in various paragraphs of the SEND COP 2015.

SEND COP 2015 Special Educational Needs and Disability Code of Practice: 0 to 25 years.

SEND Regulations 2014 The Special Educational Needs and Disability Regulations 2014 (SI 2014/1530).

SEP Special Educational Provision, in the form that this term is defined in Section 21 of the CFA 2014.

SOS!SEN SOS!SEN is an independent charity based in the United Kingdom, which offers information, advice and support to parents and carers of children with SEN and disabilities.

Upper Tribunal The court-like body that handles appeals from families or LAs in cases in which they believe that the FTT has made an error of law. The decisions of the Upper Tribunal establish binding principles for the FTT.

Young person/people A person or people who is/are over compulsory school age but under 25, as defined in Section 83(2) of the CFA 2014.

PART 1: EHCPs, their purpose, history and more

Chapter 1:
What is an EHCP?

Introduction

This chapter explores the definition of an **education, health and care plan** (EHCP), and aims to demystify its core concepts. It begins with explanations and relevant quotations from the law to set the stage. The discussion then explores situations in which it is essential to obtain an EHCP and provide a short overview of the process involved. A useful table breaks down the must-haves for each EHCP section.

It is important to bear in mind that, except for Section A, it is not the parents' or young person's responsibility to write the EHCP. This chapter offers a closer look at the collaborative process, explaining how families can contribute to creating an effective plan.

As the chapter wraps up, there is a visualisation exercise to help you to imagine how all sections of the plan connect.

EHCP definition

Children and young people with **special educational needs** (SEN) receive an EHCP when it is determined that they need extra help. This typically occurs when their nursery, school or college cannot provide all the support they require.

That extra help is called **special educational provision** (SEP) and its required scope for each particular child or young person is determined following an EHC needs assessment, which is done by the **local authority** (LA).

The EHCP for a child or young person is prepared and maintained by the LA for the area where they live. When a child or young person with an EHCP moves to an area that falls under a different LA, the plan must be transferred. Unfortunately, quite often this transfer does not occur automatically, and it is advisable to inform the new LA about the relocation.

EHCPs are important legal documents. They are made and looked after according to the rules set out in the Children and Families Act 2014 (CFA 2014).

You can find a definition of the EHCP in Section 37 of the CFA 2014:

"(2) For the purposes of this Part, an EHC plan is a plan specifying –

    a. the child's or young person's special educational needs;

    b. the outcomes sought for him or her;

    c. the special educational provision required by him or her;

    d. any health care provision reasonably required by the learning difficulties and disabilities which result in him or her having special educational needs;

    e. in the case of a child or a young person aged under 18, any social care provision which must be made for him or her by the local authority as a result of section 2 of the Chronically Sick and Disabled Persons Act 1970 (as it applies by virtue of Section 28A of that Act);

    f. any social care provision reasonably required by the learning difficulties and disabilities which result in the child or young person having special educational needs, to the extent that the provision is not already specified in the plan under paragraph (e).

(3) An EHC plan may also specify other health care and social care provision reasonably required by the child or young person."

What are SEN and SEP?

Part II of this book explores the concepts of SEN and SEP in greater depth. For now, let's consider the legal definitions to establish a basic understanding.

The definition of SEN is in Section 20(1) of the CFA 2014:

"A child or young person has special educational needs if he or she has a learning difficulty or a disability which calls for special educational provision to be made for him or her."

There are two elements to this definition:

- the child or young person must have a learning difficulty or a disability; and

- this learning difficulty or disability must require the provision of SEP to them.

The term "learning difficulty" is explained in Section 20 of the CFA 2014. For children and young people of compulsory school age or older (but under 25), it means that they find learning much harder than most others their age.

The same concept applies to younger children who are not yet old enough to go to school. However, consideration of it involves looking ahead and asking if the child is likely to have this difficulty when they reach compulsory school age.

If the main reason why a child is having trouble is that they speak a different language at home to the one they are taught in school, this is not considered a learning difficulty.

The term "disability" is not defined in the CFA 2014. Instead, it is found in Section 6(1) of the Equality Act 2010 (EqA 2010). Disability is defined as a condition, whether physical or mental, that significantly and for a long time affects a person's ability to do everyday things. It is worth pointing out that the CFA 2014 is specifically concerned with learning disabilities, whereas the EqA 2010 is concerned with disabilities in a much wider sense.

A child or young person may have either a learning difficulty or a disability, or both. They are only eligible for additional educational support under the EHCP if they require extra help in the form of SEP.

The definition of SEP is in Section 21 of the CFA 2014:

"(1) "Special educational provision", for a child aged two or more or a young person, means educational or training provision that is additional to, or different from, that made generally for others of the same age in

a. mainstream schools in England,

b. maintained nursery schools in England,

c. mainstream post-16 institutions in England, or

d. places in England at which relevant early years education is provided.

(2) "Special educational provision", for a child aged under two, means educational provision of any kind."

It is important to note that the training or education provision that a child or young person receives should be something more than – or different from – what most children their age receive in schools across England.

In Section 21 of the CFA 2014, there is another important part (subsection (5)), which says:

"Health care provision or social care provision which educates or trains a child or young person is to be treated as special educational provision (instead of health care provision or social care provision)."

As discussed earlier, a child or young person can get help through an EHCP if they have a learning difficulty or a disability that requires SEP. Notably, services related to health or social care can be considered SEP if they meet the criteria in the above definition – ie, they educate or train. Take speech and language therapy, for example. It is often seen as SEP because it educates or trains a child or young person, even though it might seem to be a healthcare service at first glance.

When is an EHCP required?

Not every child or young person who encounters difficulty is entitled to the legal benefits (including the EHCP) that are outlined in the CFA 2014. To make things clearer, all children and young people can be grouped into four categories based on their specific situations, as shown in Table 1.

Table 1: Determining EHCP eligibility according to the needs of children and young people

No	Group of children or young people	SEN		Can SEP be arranged without an EHCP?	Needs an EHCP?
		Has learning difficulty and/or disability?	Needs SEP?		
1	Typically developing children and young people with a wide range of abilities who **do not have learning difficulties or disabilities**	No	No	Not applicable	No
2	Children and young people with **learning difficulties or disabilities (or both) who do not need SEP** as they can receive support within the standard provision for their age group in mainstream settings in England – in the case of a disability, they are guarded against discrimination and have the right to reasonable adjustments under the EqA 2010	Yes	No	Not applicable	No

3	Children and young people with **learning difficulties or disabilities who have SEN and their conditions necessitate SEP** – however, the schools or post-16 institutions they attend can provide within the resources normally available the necessary support **without the need for EHCPs**	Yes	Yes	Yes	No
4	Children and young people with **learning difficulties or disabilities who have SEN, and their conditions necessitate SEP,** and the schools or post-16 institutions that they attend are unable to provide the required support – therefore, **it is essential that SEP be organised for them through EHCPs**	Yes	Yes	No	Yes

How can EHCPs be obtained?

According to the CFA 2014, the LA cannot grant an EHCP unless the child or young person has undergone the EHC needs assessment process. Although the EHC needs assessment is not the main focus of this book, let's take a moment to explore it as the background to obtaining the EHCP.

Many children and young people with special needs attend regular nurseries and schools. These educational settings offer assistance, commonly known as SEN support, through the use of their available resources. However, in some instances, this help may not be enough. In such cases, the LA has to take certain steps to figure out what the extra needs are and to address them.

Think of these steps as links in a chain. Each of them is necessary to ensure that the required support is guaranteed by law (all references are to sections in the CFA 2014).

Section 22

The LA must make sure it knows about all the children and young people in its area who may need extra help in school because they have SEN or a disability. This includes very young children who are not yet in school.

Section 24

If the LA identifies a child or young person as potentially having SEN, or if someone informs them about a child or young person who might have SEN, then the LA has to take further responsibility and decide whether an EHC needs assessment is required. It is important to note that this only happens if the child or young person has special educational requirements, not just health or care needs (even if they are serious).

Section 36

If the LA thinks the child or young person might have SEN and might need SEP, they must do the EHC needs assessment. A child's parent, a young person, or a school or college also has the right to request that this be done.

Section 37

After the EHC needs assessment is completed, if it is clear from the information collected that the child or young person needs extra support, then the LA must make sure that an EHCP is drawn up and kept up to date.

Section 42

For a child or young person with an EHCP, the LA must secure SEP as specified in the plan.

If visuals might be helpful, you can find a diagram of the timelines for the EHC needs assessment process in Paragraph 9.44 of the Special Educational Needs and Disability Code of Practice 2015 (SEND COP 2015). You can also find timelines and advice by visiting the website of the charity Independent Provider of Special Education Advice (IPSEA), which has a page dedicated to EHC needs assessments. There you can find a wealth of useful advice about various stages of the process.

Another charity, SOS!SEN, has a website that provides a range of resources. They include frequently asked questions, an EHC needs assessment information sheet and template letter, a detailed booklet explaining the process, and access to a recorded webinar that offers valuable insights.

You can find links to each website in the "online resources" section at the end of this book.

Why is obtaining an EHCP significant?

Obtaining an EHCP is important because having it grants legal entitlements and protections, which can be enforced through an appeal to the tribunal or judicial review (see pp.35-38 for more details). Having an EHCP means that the LA is legally bound to secure the SEP specified in the plan and to fund the fees for the school named in Section I.

An EHCP also provides parents or the young person with a conditional right to choose their preferred school or college. The LA must consider their preference and, unless there are statutory exceptions, comply with the request. Further information about the educational setting nomination process is available on pp.105-112.

Writing an EHCP: what is involved in the process?

In simple terms, except for Section A, the LA writes the draft EHCP and is the arbiter of all amendments.

There are specific situations in which the parents and young people will be invited to review the draft EHCP:

- upon the initial receipt of the draft EHCP from the LA following the EHC needs assessment or following a statutory re-assessment; and

- when an EHCP, accompanied by the suggested amendments, is provided by the LA after an annual review or during any other instance when the LA proposes to amend the plan.

Even though it is the LA who writes the draft EHCP, and not the parents or young people, there are options for families to provide feedback, make representations, and request amendments. The intention is that the writing process will evolve through the collaborative efforts of all parties involved in preparing an individualised EHCP for a child or young person.

When you receive the draft EHCP, you are not required immediately to accept the LA's proposals. There are a few different ways to approach the process of producing the EHCP.

Initially, the LA prepares a draft EHCP based on the EHC needs assessment, which deems the plan necessary. Many LAs use their own EHCP templates. Subsequently, the LA can amend the plan to accommodate the changing needs of the child or young person.

When the draft plan is sent to the parents or young person, they have the right to share their thoughts about it (Section 38(2)(b)(i) of the CFA 2014). They also have the right to request that the plan names a specific school or institution that the child or young person wishes to attend (Section 38(2)(b)(ii) of the CFA 2014).

In accordance with Regulations 13(1)(a)(ii) and 22(2)(c)(iii) of the SEND Regulations 2014, a child's parent or a young person can request a meeting with an LA officer to discuss the draft plan.

Regulations 13(1)(a) and 22(2)(c) of the SEND Regulations 2014 grant at least 15 days in which to examine and respond to the draft plan. If there is a disagreement concerning any aspect of the plan, use this time to communicate your feedback and suggest necessary amendments. Parents and young people can give their input by either proposing changes or offering their comments.

It is crucial to submit any comments or questions within this 15-day period. If you need more time, you should ask the LA to give it to you. If you fail to notify the LA within the 15-day timeframe, your lack of response may be considered acceptance. This may lead the LA to finalise the plan without further input.

Once you submit your comments, you may negotiate with the LA to agree on a change or find a compromise. If the negotiation is successful, then you may not need to proceed any further. Keep in mind that the LA may decline some of or all your suggested changes.

There are paths you can take to address any lingering disagreements. The first option to explore is mediation, which you should keep in mind on the way to a tribunal. When parents or young people receive the final plan, they will be given information about mediation options. Although participation in pre-tribunal mediation is voluntary, compulsory consideration of mediation is typically required (you will need to obtain a mediation certificate to confirm this). Mediation can address health, social care, or education aspects of the plan.

If you choose mediation, a mediator, the LA, parents (or young person, as applicable) and relevant professionals will participate. Parents or young people can involve a solicitor or advocate, and schools can join if that is considered beneficial.

During mediation, the parties discuss issues, aiming for an agreement. If an agreement is not reached, you may decide to file an appeal to the tribunal. The tribunal judges will evaluate evidence from both sides in order to determine what is best for the child or young person in terms of the plan's contents. In the appeal process, parties will incorporate proposed amendments into the "working document", which is a draft EHCP used to track changes. Further information about the tribunal appeals is available on on pp.35-38.

What should be included in EHCPs?

EHCPs do not have a fixed format. There are plans to create a national template for EHCPs. In early 2023, the United Kingdom's government stated this intention in their SEND and Alternative Provision Improvement Plan. The "EHCP Reform Team" at the Department of Education is working on this template and it is currently being tested in areas involved in the SEND Change Programme. The website link to information about the proposed reforms can be found in the "online resources" section at the end of this book.

It is important to note that the SEND Change Programme cannot change the existing law. LAs may ask parents and young people to try new things, but they cannot introduce rules that go against the existing legislation. Even if there are local pilot reforms, the children's and young people's rights stay the same. Adherence to legal obligations on that account will remain mandatory for LAs. Parents can continue to rely on the existing legal framework, and the SEND tribunal will continue to uphold it.

Although no set template for EHCPs exists yet, there are clear rules in Regulation 12 of the SEND Regulations 2014 that explain what the LA must include in the plan. These are organised in specific sections that are marked with letters (Table 2).

Table 2: ECHP content requirements according to Regulation 12 of the SEND Regulations 2014

Section	Content
A	The views, interests and aspirations of the child and parents or the young person
B	The child's or young person's SEN
C	The child's or young person's healthcare needs that relate to their SEN
D	The child's or young person's social care needs that relate to their SEN or to a disability
E	The outcomes sought for the child or young person
F	The SEP that is required by the child or young person
G	Any healthcare provision that is reasonably required to address the learning difficulties or disabilities that result in the child or young person having SEN
H1	Any social care provision that must be made for the child or young person according to Section 2 of the Chronically Sick and Disabled Persons Act 1970 (CSDPA 1970)
H2	Any other social care provision that is reasonably required to address the learning difficulties or disabilities that result in the child or young person having SEN
I	The name of the school, maintained nursery school, post-16 institution or other institution to be attended by the child or young person and the type of that institution or – in cases in which the name of a school or other institution is not specified in the EHCP – the type of school or other institution to be attended by the child or young person
J	In cases in which any SEP is to be secured by a direct payment as part of the personal budget, the SEN and outcomes to be met by the direct payment should be set out here
K	The advice and information obtained must be set out in appendices to the EHCP

You can find guidelines regarding the content of each section of the EHCP in the SEND COP 2015; they are shown in the table that is in Paragraph 9.69. This table is referred to in later discussions within this book, in which I describe each of the specific sections.

Since the LA writes the EHCP, you may wonder why it is beneficial for the parents and young people to know the content guidelines for each section. Understanding the purpose of each section will help you zoom in on what you are looking for when you review the LA's draft. You will know what to track down, what (if anything) is missing, and can point directly to the language in the SEND COP 2015 when sending feedback or amendment requests to the LA.

'Picture this' exercise

It can feel like the contents of the EHCP are a lot to take in. To help you better understand, it can be useful to try a technique called visualisation. This is a process whereby you create images in your mind as you read. It can help you to grasp and remember things better.

Think of an EHCP as though it were an interesting book. Each section of the plan is a part of that book and, together, they tell the story of the child's or young person's education.

There are 11 parts to explore, labelled from A to K.

Section A sets the scene, much like an engaging introduction. It introduces the child's or young person's background, strengths and aspirations.

Sections B to **D** act as the foundational chapters, in which the protagonist's character and the plot of the story are built. All three sections are focused on presenting the child's and young person's requirements.

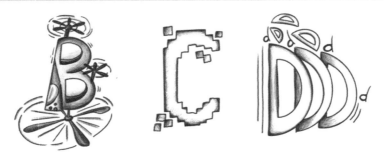

Section B meticulously records all their education needs and thereby offers an in-depth exploration of their difficulties.

Section C addresses any relevant health aspects and thus provides crucial information on medical challenges.

Section D is focused on the social care requirements that relate to the education needs.

Section E outlines the desired outcomes or goals to be achieved. It serves as a point of reference for other parts of the book.

In **Section F**, the plot thickens. Here, the EHCP reveals the plan of action that has been designed to address the education needs. It is effectively the heart of the story, in which the supporting characters – including teachers and others who help children to learn – come together to create a nurturing and inclusive environment. Section F outlines the specific support services, therapies or interventions that will be provided to help the child or young person to flourish in education. Whether it is through the provision of specialist teaching, speech and language therapy, occupational therapy, or additional teaching help, this section showcases the roadmap to success that has been specifically drawn for the child or young person.

Sections G, **H1** and **H2** comprehensively explain any healthcare and social support that is to be provided.

Section I is the grand finale. It is time to unveil the school placement that will meet all the child's or young person's needs and be able to deliver the required support.

Sections J and **K** can be likened to the supplementary materials that enhance the narrative.

A personal budget is explained in Section J. Such a budget is optional but, if it is included, it requires careful writing.

Lastly, Section K represents the technical part; it contains copies of all the advice and information that has been gathered during the EHC needs assessment and all relevant updates.

Have you tried to picture how your EHCP book might look? Do you see it with a modern and stylish design, maybe with cool fonts and bright colours? Or do you see it more as a classic, with fancy details and a timeless style like those of old books? Your EHCP book might look like an exciting adventure, a travel guide, or a technical manual with lots of information to explore. Or – who knows? – maybe you envisage it as a cookbook serving up a feast of ideas and solutions. You can imagine your EHCP book to look and feel however you want.

The purpose of this exercise is to help you remember how the different sections work together. This is vital if you want to improve your understanding of EHCPs. Part II of this book will explore how to get the plan-writing on the right track.

Take a moment

Take a moment to reflect on what you have just read.

How familiar were you with EHCPs before you read this chapter?

Were there any aspects of this chapter that stood out to you as interesting or new?

This page is for your thoughts and ideas, so feel free to write down anything that comes to mind.

Chapter 2:
History, laws and enforcement

Introduction

Chapter 2 examines the historical background and legal foundations of the EHCP, as well as practical ways in which its contents are enforced. This knowledge provides an important foundation for Part II of the book, which discusses how to write particular sections of the plan.

The chapter begins with a historical overview that covers key milestones in the establishment of the current framework. It explains the sources of law and their significance in the SEN area.

Next, the chapter explores various enforcement aspects and offers insights into how specific sections of an EHCP can be put into action.

In conclusion, it categorises EHCP sections into three groups based on different levels of enforcement power. This categorisation forms the basis for further discussion in this book.

From past to present: a brief history of EHCPs

Now and then, you might stumble upon practices that might seem a bit odd. That is because they come from old ways of doing things.

However, if you know the history, you are more likely to recognise and reconcile such situations. You will also not be surprised when you encounter fragments of old laws that are still relevant in certain circumstances.

EHCPs have a significant history. It is not a new idea to provide support for children and young people with special needs by using a document that explains their requirements. Over time, these documents have undergone several development milestones that have shaped their evolution.

Education Act 1981

The Education Act 1981 introduced the concept of a "statement of special educational needs" (SEN statement). These statements were legal documents prepared by the local authority, outlining the necessary support and provisions for children with special educational needs. They specified the type of school and support services to be provided.

Education Act 1993

The Education Act 1993 superseded the Education Act 1981 and strengthened the provisions for children with special educational needs. The new Act shifted the responsibility for co-ordinating special education to the local authorities, regardless of the school type. It introduced a code of practice for the identification and assessment of needs, revised the procedures to be used to assess needs and resources, and established a tribunal system for appeals. Parents gained legal recourse to challenge assessment and statementing decisions, with the local authority's appeals panels replaced by independent tribunals.

Education Act 1996

The EA 1996 replaced the Education Act 1993 but preserved provisions concerning children with special educational needs.

Special Educational Needs and Disability Act 2001

This Act was aimed at promoting inclusion and equal opportunities for children with disabilities or special educational needs. It introduced a duty on schools to make reasonable adjustments in order to accommodate the needs of disabled pupils.

Children Act 2004

The Act established the framework for the "Every Child Matters" policy, which was focused on improving outcomes for all children. It emphasised multi-agency collaboration and highlighted the need for integrated planning and provision of services.

Children and Families Act 2014

This Act marked a notable shift by introducing the EHCP as a substitute for the SEN statements. The coverage of the EHCP was extended to include individuals up to 25 years old. The Act outlines the processes, responsibilities and principles that should underpin EHC needs assessments, EHCP planning, and reviews. The SEND COP 2015, which compliments the Act, offers statutory guidance for the implementation of the legislation.

Legal framework

In England, there are multiple sources of law. In simple terms, a "source of law" is like a place where laws and rules come from. It is where people get the guidelines that tell them what they can and cannot do. Each source has its own level of importance and understanding them helps individuals to know what to follow and what they can expect in different situations.

The sources of law have their own hierarchy. It is like a ranking system, where some sources have more importance than others. At the top are the most crucial ones, such as Acts of Parliament, building the foundation of the legal system. Lower sources may provide additional information or guidance but have less authority. This hierarchy helps to determine which rules or laws carry more weight and should be followed in specific situations.

The main sources of law in the area of SEN are listed below.

Primary legislation (Acts of Parliament)

These acts, also known as statutes, are legally binding. This means that they compel LAs and other involved parties to comply with their provisions, and any non-compliance is unlawful. The CFA 2014 is the main piece of legislation that is relevant to the purpose of this book. It outlines the legal rights of children and young people with SEN to receive education support. The EqA 2010 is another important law that must be taken into account when it comes to children and young people with disabilities. Some sections of the EA 1996 – for example, those concerning free transport to school – still remain in effect, as do key definitions such as "child" and "compulsory school age".

Common law

Common law refers to law made by judges through their decisions.

Law evolves as people bring cases to court in order to address uncertainties or gaps in the rules. The way judges understand what the law means can become a part of the law itself, and this is called "case law". Much of the case law that matters in this area was made when the system set up under the EA 1996 was in place. If the words in the old and new laws are the same (or pretty similar), the legal decisions about SEN statements are still important for us to understand how the law works for EHCPs. That is because, most of the time, the law tries to keep things the same – unless the CFA 2014 provides a good reason to change them.

In this book, you will find complete names of court cases that established certain principles and rules. When you liaise with the LA, you can mention these cases by their names to support your arguments, just like you would refer to sections and paragraphs in the statutes. Sometimes a new case creates a new rule or modifies an old one. The Noddy No-Nonsense Guide to SEN Law is a helpful place to check whether something has changed and if there are any new decisions about the topic you are interested in. You can find the website links in the "online resources" section at the end of this book.

Secondary legislation

These are rules set by ministers (or other bodies) under powers given to them by an Act of Parliament.

Regulations typically provide specific details and instructions for the implementation of the rules set out in statutes. If there are any inconsistencies between the two, the statutes take precedence. In the context of this book, the regulations most relevant to the subject matter are the SEND Regulations 2014, which serve as the principal framework that supports and supplements the CFA 2014.

Statutory guidance

This is official guidance on how to follow the law.

In the area of SEN, official guidance comes in the form of a code of practice, the SEND COP 2015, which provides advice on the duties of LAs, schools and other agencies regarding children and young people with SEN or disabilities. If there is a difference between what the law (statutes and regulations) and the code say, the law takes precedence.

In cases in which the code uses "must" to outline a duty, it means that it indicates obligations that are compulsory under the CFA 2014 or SEND Regulations 2014. On the other hand, the word "should" in the code indicates statutory guidance. LAs are required to pay attention to it and follow it, unless there is a very good reason not to.

Legal enforcement

Now that you have a better understanding of the sources of law, consider how the laws are put into action and enforced. In England, there are several primary avenues by which individuals can challenge decisions made by the LAs regarding EHCPs.

LA complaint procedure

LAs have established complaint procedures that allow parents and young people to raise concerns about an LA's handling of EHCP matters. This can be a less formal way to address issues before complainants consider other channels.

IPSEA's website offers a valuable resource in the form of model complaint letters that are tailored to various situations. These letters serve as effective templates with which to address a wide range of concerns related to SEN.

Complaint to the ombudsman

If you are not happy with the response to your complaint, you can take it further. You can bring your concerns to the Local Government and Social Care Ombudsman, who handles complaints against LAs, or the Parliamentary and Health Services Ombudsman, who deals with complaints against healthcare organisations.

Appeal to tribunal

If the issue specifically relates to the content of the EHCP, an appeal should be made to the First-Tier Tribunal (FTT) (also known as the "SEND tribunal", "SENDIST" or simply the "tribunal"). Since this book is focused primarily on the content of the plan, it is helpful to take a slightly closer look at what can be appealed.

Education sections (B, F, and I)

Regarding the contents of the EHCP, appeals can be initiated concerning:

- the description of SEN in the EHCP (Section 51(2)(c)(i) of the CFA 2014);
- the description of SEP in the EHCP (Section 51(2)(c)(ii) of the CFA 2014);
- the refusal to change the name of the school in the EHCP to the school of parental preference (Section 51(2)(c)(iii) of the CFA 2014); and
- the failure to name a school in the EHCP (Section 51(2)(c)(iv) of the CFA 2014).

This means that the contents of all the education sections (B, F and I) can be appealed. Typically, when there is a dispute over the choice of a named school, all three sections are contested. If the disagreement revolves solely around SEP, then usually only Sections B and F are challenged.

Health and social care sections (C, D, G, H1, and H2)

According to Section 21(5) of the CFA 2014, healthcare provision (normally found in Section G) or social care provision (normally found in Section H) that "educates or trains" a child or young person is to be treated as SEP and, therefore, should be specified in Section F of the EHCP. An appeal is possible if this provision has been placed incorrectly in the wrong part of the plan.

There may also be situations that are a bit confusing. Although there are requirements regarding the content of each of the ECHP's sections, the exact way in which these sections are organised and presented is not strictly defined by the regulations. Each LA has the freedom to interpret and create its EHCPs in its own manner. By way of example, all the provision sections (F, G and H) could be combined in a table that is linked to the outcomes in Section E. This approach can create confusion, especially when users of the EHCP try to distinguish between SEP (which is appealable) and health and social care provision (which is not). If SEN or SEP descriptions are in the wrong places in the EHCP, pursuing an appeal is an option but it may be complicated and require in-depth legal evaluation.

Otherwise, the tribunal can make only "non-binding recommendations" on health and social care (Sections C, D, G, H1, and H2). These types of appeals are referred to as "extended appeals" and can be pursued only if you appeal simultaneously against the education sections of the EHCP (Sections B, F and/or I).

Other sections (A, E, J, and K)

Unfortunately, you cannot appeal against the contents of these sections. However, there is a general power granted to the tribunal under Regulation 43(1) of the SEND Regulations 2014 to "correct any deficiencies" in the plan. This power could be used to, for example, change the outcomes so that they align with the revised SEP, even though there is not a specific appeal avenue for Section E. Similarly, although you cannot challenge what is in Section K before the tribunal, this content may be changed if you successfully challenge the education sections and that leads to changes to Sections B and F that render information in other parts (such as Section K) inadequate. Then the tribunal can decide to have those sections updated too.

Given that parents and young people make direct input regarding the content in Section A, it is rare for families to challenge this particular section.

Judicial review

In certain situations, you can consider a judicial review, which is essentially a check and balance in the legal system. At a judicial review, a court reviews and evaluates decisions and actions that public bodies have taken to ensure they have followed the rules and laws.

The aim is to stop those in power from overstepping their authority or acting unfairly.

A judicial review is not appropriate for challenging the content of the EHCP. It might be an option in some education-related situations, such as the LA's failure to secure the SEP specified in Section F or failure to place the child or young person at the school or institution named in Section I.

Keep in mind that judicial review is a "remedy of last resort" and, as such, you should not pursue it if there are other opportunities for appeal. What this means is that if there is a statutory appeals process (such as the tribunal appeal for EHCPs, procedures to challenge the decisions on school admissions and exclusions, or internal appeals regarding certain transport decisions), then you should not use judicial review but instead follow that specific appeal procedure to challenge relevant decisions.

SOS!SEN provides a service to assist with the preparation of pre-action protocols, which is an important first step in starting the judicial review process. Should the matter remain unresolved at this stage, you can inquire whether you are eligible for legal aid and ask for recommendations from legal professionals who have expertise in handling such cases.

How EHCP sections are covered in this book

The key point to remember is that different sections of the EHCP present different opportunities for appeal. In this book, the EHCP sections are categorised as education, health, social care, and all other sections.

If you look at them in this way, you can allocate your time and resources efficiently for each section, recognising their significance and potential impact.

Take a moment

Take a moment to reflect on what you have just read.

Are there any aspects of EHCP history, laws or enforcement that have sparked your curiosity or concern?

How does the information about the tribunal's role in the enforcement of EHCPs align with or challenge your previous understanding?

Write any thoughts and ideas that come to mind.

Chapter 3: Gathering information and advice

Introduction

Take a moment to appreciate something truly important, which is that the quality of an EHCP significantly depends on the advice and information that are used to write it.

Reports from experts are often copied by the LA exactly, word for word, in the text of an EHCP. This means that, when preparing the plan's draft, the LA may be reluctant to make any changes or edits to the report's language. Therefore, the advice and information that is collected should offer comprehensive insight into the child's or young person's needs and the support they require.

This chapter explores the initial steps in the gathering of relevant information. It also covers how these findings pave the way towards in-depth discussions with experts and, ultimately, towards seeking the assistance needed to create a well-informed, actionable EHCP.

Identification of SEN

It is best to begin by exploring the main points and guidance with regard to identifying SEN.

Children who have not reached compulsory school age

Health professionals play a crucial role in the identification of young children who have SEN. If a health body believes that a child who is below compulsory school age has (or probably has) SEN, they must inform the child's parents and bring the child to the attention of the LA (Section 23 of the CFA 2014).

In early-years settings, if a child's rate of progress leads to concerns about them falling behind expected levels, practitioners should gather comprehensive information about their learning and development.

If specialist advice has been sought from outside the setting, this should also be considered during the determination of whether a child has SEN. All this information should be put together and carefully examined, with input from parents.

When the LA identifies – or is informed of – a child who may have SEN, they become responsible for further consideration of the child's needs (Section 24 of the CFA 2014). This means that, in consultation with the child's parents, they must assess whether an EHC needs assessment (Section 36 of the CFA 2014) and perhaps an EHCP (Section 37 of the CFA 2014) is required.

Under the CFA 2014, there is no differentiation between children who are under two years old and those aged two to five, when it comes to EHC needs assessments. The criteria are the same regardless of a child's age. Any child can undergo an EHC needs assessment and potentially receive an EHCP.

Children of compulsory school age

SEN can be identified in some children at an early age. For others, difficulties may become apparent as they grow. All people who work with children should be alert to potential difficulties, and schools are required to have a clear process to identify and address SEN.

This involves the evaluation of each child's skills and progress, with consideration of past information and recognition of potential disabilities. Ongoing assessments, with a focus on the provision of tailored teaching, are also important.

A child may struggle at school in different ways. They may find it difficult to understand what they are being taught or they may become restless or inattentive. That may be fine if the child is learning and getting good grades but the social side of school is just exhausting and overwhelming for them. Children might find the noise overwhelming and interactions challenging, so it becomes hard for them to connect with other children. Physical disabilities, such as sight or hearing loss, may also contribute to the challenges.

Disruptive behaviour does not automatically imply SEN. A thorough assessment is needed to explore potential causes. Professionals should also be aware of external factors such as bullying or bereavement, which can affect a child's well-being. While these events may not lead to SEN, they can alter a child's mental health and overall welfare and require schools to address the associated short-term needs.

Schools often need to take the initiative to understand and provide the necessary support. This support, commonly known as SEN support, is mandated by Section 66 of the CFA 2014. This section imposes a "best endeavours" duty on maintained nurseries and mainstream schools to implement the SEP that the child or young person needs.

Schools (with the exception of independent ones) currently receive delegated funding of up to £6,000 each year for each child who has SEN support. This funding is intended to meet the required needs and provide support; however, it is not ring-fenced for a particular pupil, which can present challenges in practice.

Schools are then required to follow the so-called "assess, plan, do and review" process. They assess the needs, plan the support, implement the support, and then review the support to see whether it is working. They then evaluate whether adjustments, further assessments, or specialist involvement are needed.

In practice, the SEN support process is often carried out by schools through the drawing-up of documents known by various names such as individual learning plans or individual education plans. Broadly, these documents outline the needs and support required. They are distributed to all the staff within the school who work with the child. Therefore, these staff should be aware of the child's needs and the support required – including in terms of tailored teaching strategies and approaches – and should deliver such support.

When professionals assess SEN in children whose first language is not English, they should consider carefully whether any lack of progress is due to language proficiency or whether it is indicative of SEN or a disability.

If a mainstream setting can address the needs of a child adequately with the resources it has available, an EHCP is not necessary. However, if they need support beyond what the school is able to offer or if a special school placement is necessary, an EHCP is typically required.

It is not necessary to have SEN support in place before requesting an EHC needs assessment. The law does not stipulate that the assessment should only be initiated after a specific number of cycles of SEN support have been tried and proven unsuccessful. However, the data gathered from SEN support can be compelling evidence of the need for SEP and, consequently, an EHCP.

The process for requesting an EHC needs assessment and an EHCP is the same for this age group as for pre-school ages.

Young people

Colleges should actively engage in the planning of young people's transitions from school to college and should anticipate their needs to ensure that they transition smoothly into college life.

Some needs may arise after a student has started their college programme. Teaching staff should collaborate with providers of specialist support to pinpoint any challenges that a young person may be facing, which may be related to SEN.

Paragraph 7.12 of the SEND COP 2015 outlines the criteria by which young people who have difficulties should be identified and supported. It emphasises that those who may have struggled in school or who are working below a certain level (that the code refers to as "below level 2") should receive extra attention.

The code's guidance, though, is that no one should assume that the student has SEN based solely on lower attainment levels compared with peers. Any potential SEN should be specifically identified and supported.

Similarly, it should not be assumed that students in higher-level courses do not have any learning difficulties or disabilities that warrant SEP.

Under the CFA 2014, the assessment process for young people mirrors that of children, except that the right to request an EHC needs assessment shifts from the parent to the young person. The criteria for issuing an EHCP for a young person align with those used in the case of a child. A plan should be issued if, after an EHC needs assessment, it is determined that SEP must be made via an EHCP.

Uncovering challenges, strengths and aspirations

Parents can play a significant role in uncovering their child's strengths, challenges and aspirations by actively engaging in observation, communication and reflection. Each child is unique, so there is a lot to think about.

It is important to keep records. Think about what method you will use to document your observations. It should be something that aligns with your child's abilities and your comfort level, such as writing in a traditional notebook, using a digital device to record audio or video, using a specialised app, or a combination of these.

Organise the observations into distinct categories to reveal patterns and trends. A good place to begin might be the developmental milestones provided by the National Health Service (NHS) on its website. You can use these milestones, which are based on a child's age, to compare an average child's abilities with those of your child.

When it comes to education, a wide range of factors can lead to difficulties. Neurological differences such as autism or ADHD often come into play. Special needs can be related to health.

Many children's challenges are multi-faceted, so the term "complex needs" is often used to describe them. It helps if you look at the child as a whole and take into account all aspects of their characteristics and needs. Below, I provide some tips on what to pay attention to. This will help you get the most from your records when you need them later on.

It can be beneficial to organise your notes by grouping them according to the "areas of need" specified in the EHCP. As stated in Paragraph 5.32 of the SEND COP 2015, children's SEN are usually categorised into four broad categories, which are considered here.

Communication and interaction

Children and young people may have communication difficulties. This may be because they find it hard to express themselves, to understand what others are saying, or to follow the common rules of how to converse with others. Each child's communication needs are unique and might change over time, affecting how they use language and interact with others.

Tips: You can spot signs of communication and interaction difficulties in your child by watching out for things such as how they talk, play, and act around others. Keep an eye on how they use words, how they get along with friends, and how they play creatively. Also, notice whether they do the same things over and over or get upset a lot.

Cognition and learning

Children and young people might need extra support with their learning if they are not catching on as quickly as their friends are. Learning difficulties can vary hugely. Some kids may have moderate learning difficulties; this phrase means that they need help with most subjects and may have trouble with moving and talking. Others may have profound and multiple learning difficulties, meaning they face really tough challenges when learning, along with physical disabilities or problems with their senses. Then there are specific learning difficulties, such as dyslexia or dyscalculia, which mainly affect certain parts of learning (eg, reading or maths).

Tips: You can help by looking for signs of whether your child is facing learning challenges. Keep an eye on how they learn compared with other children. Notice if they have trouble remembering things, paying attention, or staying organised. If you see any changes in how they learn over time, that is important too.

Social, emotional and mental health

Children and young people can go through many different feelings and struggles, which can show up in various ways. Some might become quiet or distant, whereas others may act out or be disruptive. These behaviours may be linked in some cases to mental health issues such as anxiety, depression, self-harm, or problems with substances or eating.

Tips: You can keep an eye out for certain things – for instance, you may notice changes in how your child expresses feelings or whether they are spending more time alone than they did before. Be aware of any sudden changes in behaviour, sleep and appetite or of physical symptoms that have no clear cause.

Sensory and/or physical needs

Some children and young people may experience sensory integration challenges. This means that some of their senses – how they see, hear, feel, smell or taste things – do not always work smoothly. Sometimes they might feel things too strongly, such as sounds being too loud or clothes feeling scratchy. At other times, they might not notice things as much as you expect; they may not react when someone calls their name, for example.

Tips: These challenges can make it tricky for the child or young person to access education facilities. Take note if your child often over-reacts or under-reacts to things such as sounds, textures or other sensations. Also, look out for any behaviours they use to cope, such as avoiding noisy places or seeking out certain sensory experiences.

From Year 9 (typically around the age of 13), the significance of the mentioned areas of SEN remains, but the emphasis starts to shift towards preparing for adulthood. Chapter 8 of the SEND COP 2015 goes into some depth about this transition and includes a list of considerations to take into account.

Here is a short overview:

Support to prepare for higher education and/or employment

It is important to start exploring interests, setting goals and preparing for the future. The planning should include discussions of career options, visits to colleges and universities if higher education is a possibility, and consideration of internships or work experience.

Tips: Keep track of your child's goals and share them with their school to see whether these aspirations align with what the school hopes they can achieve. Identify the components that should be included in their study programme to best prepare them for adult life.

Support to prepare for independent living

This should involve thinking about the young person's future living arrangements, including their preferences regarding where and with whom they want to live, as well as the necessary support.

Tips: Seek information about local housing choices, assistance in finding accommodation, housing benefits and social care support.

Support to maintain good health in adult life

Well-planned transitions are crucial to promote the young person's health in adult life. This requires reflection on reasonable adjustments that will boost mental and physical health, planning for the transition to adult health services, arranging eye and dental check-ups, evaluation of the curriculum's impact on a healthy lifestyle, and signposting the need for continuing health and care arrangements.

Tips: Ensure the continued good health of children and young people as they grow by planning the transition from specialist paediatric care to adult healthcare. It is important to help the young person to understand which healthcare professionals will support them in adulthood and to ensure that these professionals are aware of any learning difficulties or disabilities.

Support to participate in society

This should involve consideration of ways to help the young person to expand their circle of friends, foster connections within and outside school/college, explore additional community activities and identify opportunities for them to contribute actively and become recognised, such as through volunteering.

Tips: Take the initiative by researching social and community activities. It would be good to get a clear plan of how a child or young person could be supported in developing and maintaining friendships and relationships.

Identification of SEP

For a child or young person to be recognised as having SEN, two conditions must be met: they must have a learning difficulty or a disability and it must require SEP for them.

When it comes to the identification of the appropriate SEP to address the difficulties, various examples may be considered, depending on the circumstances of the case. Some are shown in the table below (Table 3), which cites important cases that laid the groundwork for the applicable principles.

Table 3: Examples of SEP, with rationale and references to court cases

SEP	Comments and case reference
Health and social care that is educational	If it meets the test in Section 21(5) of the CFA 2014 – ie, such provision must "educate" or "train" to be included as SEP.
Inclusion in a particular peer group	SEP may include provision for a non mainstream peer group. AJ v LB Croydon [2020] UKUT 246 (AAC)

Placement in a different year group	Placement of a child or young person in a year group that differs from the one aligned with their chronological age could be included as SEP. *AB v North Somerset [2010] UKUT 8 (AAC)*
Provision beyond "school hours"	If support is required beyond the regular school day, SEP may be warranted when a child or young person requires the application and transfer of skills learned within the school and classroom to their home, to social interactions, and to aid overall functioning in various aspects of life. See various pieces of case law related to a "waking day curriculum".
Psychiatric input	Psychiatric input may qualify as SEP based on specific circumstances, but it should not encompass any vague "well-being" sessions that do not contain any elements of instruction or training. *DC and DC v Hertfordshire CC [2016] UKUT 379 (AAC)*
Requirement for one-to-one work	SEP may entail a requirement for and detail the extent of one-to-one support. *L v Clarke and Somerset [1998] ELR 129*

Small group work specifications	For small group work, factors such as the size of the group and the duration and frequency of the sessions should be detailed in the SEP description. *L v Clarke and Somerset [1998] ELR 129*
Size of the class or small group teaching	SEP may encompass situations in which a child requires small group teaching or placement in classes that contain fewer pupils than those typically provided in a mainstream school. *H v Leicestershire [2000] ELR 471*
Speech and language therapy	Paragraph 9.74 of the SEND COP 2015 sums up the position on this as follows: "Speech and language therapy and other therapy provision can be regarded as either education or health care provision, or both. It could therefore be included in an EHC plan as either educational or health provision. However, since communication is so fundamental in education, addressing speech and language impairment should normally be recorded as special educational provision unless there are exceptional reasons for not doing so".

Staff qualifications and experience	SEP may include the provision of a teacher who has expertise in working with children and young people who face, for example, significant learning difficulties or language disorders. *R v Wandsworth ex parte M [1998] ELR 424*
Transport provision (in exceptional cases)	See Paragraph 9.215 of the SEND COP 2015.

The list in Table 3 is not exhaustive, and you may receive professional recommendations for other types of SEP. However, since the examples mentioned above are backed by case law, the LA would find it difficult to argue against any of them being designated as SEP.

In accordance with Section 30 of the CFA 2014, all LAs must publish specific information referred to as a "Local Offer". This document should detail all SEP the LA expects to be accessible for children and young people for whom it is responsible. If you find the Local Offer published by your LA challenging to understand or if it is difficult to locate the information you need, you can enquire directly with the LA about the available resources and funding. These details will help you to understand what can and cannot be provided without an EHCP.

Another valuable resource regarding SEP is the SEN Information Report that schools are required to publish. Please note that this requirement does not apply to independent schools.

Roles of professionals and experts

It is said that parents are the experts regarding their children. This sentiment recognises a parent's close bond and familiarity with their child.

Yet, this statement does not fully capture the complexity of a child's needs. Their experiences encompass their interactions with peers, educators and others, along with their own emotions and thoughts, which may not be apparent to even the most attentive parent.

Sometimes, a child's needs or challenges might call for specialist knowledge or professional guidance in order to gain complete understanding and to provide the right support. As you follow your child's growth milestones, if you detect any notable delays, it would be logical to seek extra guidance.

You may consider seeking advice from the following types of experts.

Paediatricians

can diagnose and offer guidance on medical aspects of SEN.

Educational psychologists

conduct assessments and provide recommendations regarding education support.

Speech and language therapists

are experts in communication disorders and help children with speech and language difficulties.

Speech and language pathologists

are similar to speech and language therapists, in that they focus on improving speech and language skills.

Occupational therapists

assist with fine motor skills, sensory processing, and activities of daily living.

Vision specialists

are experts in vision impairment and assist children with visual challenges.

Behavioural optometrists

are specialists who assess visual processing.

Audiologists

assess and treat hearing impairments.

Behavioural audiologists

are specialists who assess auditory processing.

You will probably not require every type of expert right away (and may not ever need some of them). You can also be strategic about whom to involve.

If you are seeking an expert, consider exploring these links to professional directories.

The British Psychological Society (BPS)

is a professional body for psychologists in the United Kingdom. The BPS provides resources, guidelines and support for psychologists in various fields, including educational psychology. It also plays a role in setting ethical standards and codes of conduct. You can access their directory to find educational psychologists at www.bps.org.uk/find-psychologist. This directory allows users to filter their search, facilitating the identification of professionals with experience as expert witnesses in the SEND tribunal.

The Association of Speech and Language Therapists in Independent Practice (ASLTIP)

is a professional organisation in the United Kingdom for independent speech and language therapists. ASLTIP serves as a representative body for these professionals, providing support, resources, and information related to the field. The association also offers a directory on its website (www.asltip.com/find-a-speech-therapist) to help individuals find independent speech and language therapists.

The Royal College of Occupational Therapists (RCOT)

is a professional organisation in the United Kingdom dedicated to advancing the discipline of occupational therapy. Through research and advocacy, the RCOT contributes to the enhancement of occupational therapy services and the overall health and quality of life of those who benefit from this specialised form of healthcare. The organisation offers a directory on its website (www.rcot.co.uk/about-occupational-therapy/find-occupational-therapist) for individuals seeking an expert in this area.

Bear in mind that receiving education accommodations does not depend on having a particular diagnosis. However, a diagnosis may be relevant to health services that will then provide referrals to specialists. You can ask your school to make referrals if your general practitioner (GP) is not addressing your concerns.

Even if a neurodevelopmental assessment is not feasible or your child is on a long waiting list, there are still avenues you can explore to get help with their challenges. You do not need to pinpoint the exact cause of their difficulties to explore therapies such as speech and language or occupational therapy. Assessments for therapeutic support may produce valuable and prompt results.

Consider which services are vital for your child's development at this stage. Seeking guidance from the right experts can quickly unlock possible accommodations and noticeable advancement.

As you engage with specialists, you begin to gather expert evidence to support your observations. This marks a significant milestone. It is no longer just about your personal feelings regarding the situation; your intuitive insights are complemented by informed knowledge and solid, expert perspectives. You are laying the foundation for an evidential base, which will enable you to initiate the journey of understanding your child's legal entitlements and seeking suitable accommodations.

This collection of evidence, combined with your detailed observations and developmental records, equips you to make informed decisions about the next steps. It empowers you to approach the right individuals and ask the right questions as you consider further action.

Conducting assessments and evaluations

EHC needs assessment

The essential step towards obtaining the EHCP is the EHC needs assessment. An EHCP cannot be issued without the completion of this assessment and the evidence gathered during the process will be used to draft the EHCP if the decision to grant it is made.

You can find a definition of the EHC needs assessment in Section 36(2) of the CFA 2014:

> *"An "EHC needs assessment" is an assessment of the educational, health care and social care needs of a child or young person."*

The statutory test determining whether the EHC needs assessment is required is outlined in Section36(8) of the CFA 2014:

> *"(8) The local authority must secure an EHC needs assessment for the child or young person if, after having regard to any views expressed and evidence submitted under subsection (7), the authority is of the opinion that—*
>
> > *e. the child or young person has or may have special educational needs, and*
> >
> > *f. it may be necessary for special educational provision to be made for the child or young person in accordance with an EHC plan."*

Any LA's internal policies that are more stringent or impose additional requirements beyond what is mandated by law are unlawful.

Paragraph 9.14 of the SEND COP 2015 provides examples of what the LA may need to consider when deciding whether an EHC needs assessment is necessary. This list is reproduced below to provide you with an understanding of the kind of evidence that may prove useful when pursuing an EHC needs assessment:

> ■ *evidence of the child or young person's academic attainment (or developmental milestones in younger children) and rate of progress;*

- information about the nature, extent and context of the child or young person's SEN;

- evidence of the action already being taken by the early-years provider, school or post-16 institution to meet the child or young person's SEN;

- evidence that where progress has been made, it has only been as the result of much additional intervention and support over and above that which is usually provided; and

- evidence of the child or young person's physical, emotional and social development and health needs, drawing on relevant evidence from clinicians and other health professionals and what has been done to meet these by other agencies.

- Where a young person is aged over 18, the LA must consider whether the young person requires additional time – in comparison to the majority of others of the same age who do not have SEN – to complete their education or training. Remaining in formal education or training should help young people to achieve education and training outcomes, building on what they have learned before and preparing them for adult life.

To initiate an EHC needs assessment, in some instances it may be enough to present evidence of learning difficulties and specify the assistance required. However, to justify the need for an EHCP, in most cases it becomes essential to provide details of the support already in place and explain why this may not be sufficient in the future. This could stem from a lack of progress or an indication that the current level of support is unsustainable without an EHCP in place.

In the event the LA decides to conduct the EHC needs assessment, it must seek the following advice and information according to Regulation 6(1) of the SEND Regulations 2014:

"(a) advice and information from the child's parent or the young person;

(b) educational advice and information:

 i. from the head teacher or principal of the school or post-16 or other institution that the child or young person is attending, or

> ii. where this is not available, from a person who the local authority is satisfied has experience of teaching children or young people with special educational needs, or [has] knowledge of the differing provision [that] may be called for in different cases to meet those needs, or
>
> iii. if the child or young person is not currently attending a school or post-16 or other institution and advice cannot be obtained under sub-paragraph (ii), from a person responsible for educational provision for the child or young person, and
>
> iv. if any parent of the child or young person is a serving member of Her Majesty's armed forces, also from the Secretary of State for Defence;
>
> (c) medical advice and information from a healthcare professional identified by the responsible commissioning body;
>
> (d) psychological advice and information from an educational psychologist;
>
> (e) advice and information in relation to social care;
>
> (f) advice and information from any other person the local authority thinks is appropriate;
>
> (g) where the child or young person is in or beyond Year 9, advice and information in relation to provision to assist the child or young person in preparation for adulthood and independent living; and
>
> (h) advice and information from any person the child's parent or young person reasonably requests that the local authority seek advice from."

The above list emphasises the importance of gathering a wide range of advice and information to create a comprehensive understanding of the child's or young person's needs. It suggests that the LA should consider seeking advice and information from various professionals, including education, health and social care professionals, and any other relevant experts.

Besides reports commissioned by the LA (for example, from the NHS), you can also use private reports. Even though some LAs may be hesitant to accept them, it is beneficial to let them know if you have any. If the LA does not agree to take them into account and declines to include their content in the EHCP, you can bring them up during a tribunal appeal as evidence.

The quality of an EHCP depends on the quality of the advice and information it incorporates. Reports that contain vague terms and generalisations can result in EHCPs that lack precision and effectiveness. Suggestions such as provision being delivered "as required" or through unspecified "programmes" that are "to be determined" or "explored" do not contribute significantly to the EHCP, as they lack the necessary clarity and specificity. Ideally, the language in the reports should adhere to the same writing principles that are applied in Section F of the EHCP. You can refer to the guidance on pp.88-105 for detailed explanations.

Expert advice should aim to establish clear and specific measures, rather than leaving provisions open-ended. Sometimes the LA claims that it cannot specify provision as the reports are not precise. In this situation, ask the LA to challenge the provider of the advice and seek clarification on any vagueness in reports. It will ensure that the EHCP is meaningful and beneficial for the child or young person it serves.

The SEND COP 2015 emphasises the significance of providing advice that is clear, accessible and specific (as outlined in Paragraph 9.51). This provision is quoted below in full for reference. It may be relevant to cite this if disagreements arise with the LA:

"The evidence and advice submitted by those providing it should be clear, accessible and specific. They should provide advice about outcomes relevant for the child or young person's age and phase of education and strategies for their achievement. The local authority may provide guidance about the structure and format of advice and information to be provided. Professionals should limit their advice to areas in which they have expertise. They may comment on the amount of provision they consider a child or young person requires and local authorities should not have blanket policies [that] prevent them from doing so."

To summarise, in their reports, professionals must address the needs of the child or young person, the provision that is required to meet those needs, and the outcomes they believe that provision could achieve. When professionals believe a child or young person requires specialist intervention, it is insufficient to imply vaguely what that intervention could be. They must detail the requirements explicitly and provide a clear rationale for them. There should be no room for interpretation. This should be the standard for well-structured recommendations in a high-quality report. It is becoming quite common that when a tribunal decides not to follow expert advice, the excuse given is often that the experts have not really explained their recommended support.

The LA often copies the experts' language word-for-word into the draft EHCP. Therefore, the foundation of a strong plan lies in the strength and quality of the expert evidence. This is why it is important to commence your advocacy efforts during interactions with doctors and specialists to ensure that the language and content generated in those settings are fit for purpose in order to produce an effective EHCP.

As already mentioned above, discussions about introducing a national template for EHCPs are ongoing, with selected LAs running a pilot to test it. Given the importance of professional reports, it may be worth creating a national template for the evidence presented by individual professionals as part of the EHC needs assessment. This way, we could ensure that the information and advice – based on which a child's or young person's EHCP is created – are as thorough and complete as possible and align with the legal requirements. While this point may not be the focus of national debate right now, it is worth giving some thought to.

Re-assessment

A child or young person with an existing EHCP can undergo a re-assessment to address their changing education, health and social care needs. This allows for the collection of up-to-date evidence and identification of the appropriate support required.

The legal provisions regarding re-assessment can be found in Section 44 of the CFA 2014:

> *"(2) A local authority must secure a re-assessment of the educational, health care and social care needs of a child or young person for whom it maintains an EHC plan if a request is made to it by:*
>
> a. *the child's parent or the young person, or*
>
> b. *the governing body, proprietor or principal of the school, post-16 institution or other institution which the child or young person attends.*
>
> (3) *A local authority may also secure a re-assessment of those needs at any other time if it thinks it necessary."*

The re-assessment essentially involves a fresh EHC needs assessment, which is to be carried out as soon as the LA agrees to re-assess or when mandated by law.

Following the re-assessment, the EHCP will be amended by the LA in collaboration with the parents or young person to incorporate the latest information gathered during the evaluation of needs. This will follow the same steps as the legal process for the EHC needs assessment. For a reminder on the EHCP writing and amendment process, please refer to pp.21-23 for more details.

Further reading

For those who wish to deepen their understanding of the SEN identification process, exploration of the literature in this field can greatly expand your knowledge.

The Out-of-Sync Child by Carol Kranowitz

This widely acclaimed book explores the topic of sensory processing disorder, a condition in which the sensory signals received by the brain are not processed effectively. The book provides valuable insights and practical advice on how to handle children who struggle with sensory issues.

More Than Words: A Parent's Guide to Building Interaction and Language Skills for Children with Autism Spectrum Disorder or Social Communication Difficulties **by Fern Sussman**

This highly regarded book is aimed at families that include autistic children or those with social communication difficulties. It provides practical strategies and guidance to improve communication and interaction skills.

Eyes OK, I'm OK **by Harold Wiener**

This is a comprehensive guide that is tailored for optometrists, educators and parents who seek to optimise children's visual development. It describes effective strategies for children who may not be progressing as expected in their perceptual-motor skills. The book offers invaluable insights and practical ways to nurture and enhance children's visual abilities.

Food Refusal and Avoidant Eating in Children, including those with Autism Spectrum Conditions: A Practical Guide for Parents and Professionals **by Gillian Harris and Elizabeth Shea**

This is a comprehensive guidebook written to address the challenges associated with food refusal and selective eating in children.

Like Sound Through Water: A Mother's Journey Through Auditory Processing Disorder **by Karen J Foli**

This memoir chronicles the author's emotional journey as a mother raising a child with APD. Foli provides a deeply personal account of the challenges she encountered and the triumphs and discoveries she made as she navigated the complexities of APD.

Take a moment

Take a moment to reflect on what you have just read.

What advantages might early intervention offer?

Consider how different cultural viewpoints may shape the acknowledgement of SEN and the assistance offered to individuals with SEN.

As before, use the space as you wish.

Chapter 4:
Advocacy, self-advocacy and mental capacity

Introduction

The education system is complex, and resources are usually limited. There is a vital need for someone to step up and advocate for the protection of children's and young people's rights and best interests. Mere expressions of concern may not suffice; active collaboration with teachers and professionals is essential in order to bring about meaningful change. This active kind of involvement is what is commonly known as **advocacy**.

In the context of this book, even though the LA is the body responsible for preparing and writing the EHCP, the advocacy efforts of parents, young people, and other parties involved can play a crucial role in shaping an effective EHCP and ensuring its overall success.

This chapter starts with a discussion of the core principles that guide how LAs support and involve children, young people and their families, laying the groundwork for advocacy efforts. It then explores effective strategies to assist you in expressing your views and wishes, as well as understanding and exercising your rights. In addition, specific aspects of advocacy for children and young people are examined.

Core principles that shape the local authority's duties

The following principles should be at the heart of everything the LA does for all children and young people with SEN, whether or not they have EHCPs, as it follows the CFA 2014. They also lay down a strong foundation for advocacy work.

Section 19 of the CFA 2014 outlines the core principles that an LA must consider as it performs its duties, here is its text in full.

> **"Local authority functions: supporting and involving children and young people**
>
> In exercising a function under this Part in the case of a child or young person, a local authority in England must have regard to the following matters in particular:
>
> a. the views, wishes and feelings of the child and his or her parent, or the young person;
>
> b. the importance of the child and his or her parent, or the young person, participating as fully as possible in decisions relating to the exercise of the function concerned;
>
> c. the importance of the child and his or her parent, or the young person, being provided with the information and support necessary to enable participation in those decisions;
>
> d. the need to support the child and his or her parent, or the young person, in order to facilitate the development of the child or young person and to help him or her achieve the best possible educational and other outcomes."

These principles give a clear standard by which one can measure the LA's actions and choices. By emphasising their importance, you can effectively stress the need to always follow practices that are consistent, fair and inclusive when supporting children and young people.

Take note of the phrase "must have regard" at the beginning of this section. This means the LA is obliged to take into account the points listed in (a)-(d) when it makes a decision or acts. This duty is not discretionary; it is reinforced by the use of the word "must", which indicates that the LA must adhere to what is prescribed.

Consideration of the views of the child, young person or their parents has a significant impact on the LA's duties, including tasks such as conducting EHC needs assessments, preparing and maintaining EHCPs, and naming schools and institutions in Section I. Parents and young people must be consulted on any proposed amendments to the EHCP and informed of their rights to appeal. LAs must facilitate parents' and young people's participation as fully as possible.

LAs must also prioritise children, young people, and families in their planning. They must collaborate with them to develop co-ordinated approaches through which to achieve good outcomes. Currently, there is no clear method by which a parent or young person can appeal the contents of Sections A or E to the tribunal. However, their perspectives should carry significant weight.

Disregarding input from a parent or young person, for instance, regarding Section E (outcomes), would run counter to the intent of Section 19(d). Similarly, overlooking parents' or young people's contributions to Section A would not be in line with the spirit of Section 19(a), which emphasises "wishes, views, and feelings". In such situations, a parent or young person has the option to file a complaint if the LA chooses not to consider their comments.

Furthermore, this section of the CFA 2014 emphasises "the best possible educational and other outcomes" and the need to facilitate the development and achievements of the child or young person. This need is crucial, as it sets the standard for the evaluation of the suggested support provision.

It has long been established case law in connection with SEP that children and young people are entitled to "appropriate provision" rather than the absolute "best provision", commonly known as "Rolls Royce provision". In other words, it is unreasonable for parents or young people to expect gold handrails when steel will do an excellent job. However, when the term "best" is employed here, it means striving for the highest possible outcomes.

If it can be argued that the suggested SEP will not contribute to the best possible outcomes, it is worth referencing this section to advocate for improvements in the SEP that is offered. Note that Section 19(d) does not mandate the achievement of the best possible outcomes. Rather, it requires the consideration of provision that could lead to such outcomes, alongside other factors that are within the LA's purview.

Advocacy strategies

Advocacy is a journey that demands careful consideration and smart planning, whether it is advocacy on behalf of your child, or the young person advocating for themself. The use of effective advocacy techniques can help you to navigate the education system confidently and to ensure that the right support is provided.

Here are a few strategies that you might want to think about. Self-advocates may consider which parts of this list apply to them.

Educate yourself about SEN

You should learn about the relevant laws, policies and regulations that are related to SEN. This knowledge will empower you to navigate the education system effectively.

Know your rights

Familiarise yourself with your rights as a parent of a child with SEN or as a young person with SEN. Understand the processes of requesting assessments, obtaining an EHCP, and accessing support services.

Collaborate with school staff

Build positive relationships and work collaboratively with teachers, the SENCO, and other school professionals.

Keep detailed records

Maintain organised data regarding assessments, evaluations, communications with school staff, and any other relevant documents. These records will support your advocacy efforts and provide evidence of the child's or young person's needs.

Stay informed about progress

Regularly monitor your child's progress and stay informed about their academic and social development. Ask for feedback from teachers and request updates on your child's goals and achievements.

Seek professional guidance

If necessary, seek advice from specialists such as education or health professionals. They can provide valuable insights and guidance.

Connect with other parents

Find and stay in touch with parents of other children or young people with SEN. Sharing experiences and strategies with others can be empowering and provide a sense of community and support.

Stay positive and be persistent

If you embrace a positive, persistent and focused approach towards your child's (or your own) needs, this will lead to better outcomes than would a negative outlook.

Children under 16 years old

When it comes to making decisions about EHCPs for children, the parents usually have the say. They are responsible for exercising the rights of the child. Parental responsibility typically lasts until the child turns 18 years old. However, rights under the CFA 2014 automatically transition from parents to young people when those young people reach the end of compulsory schooling, which is generally around 16 years old.

Advocates come from various backgrounds: some are legal experts, whereas others are parents of children with SEN who have walked a similar path towards obtaining the required support and can offer valuable guidance. In addition, charities play a crucial role in advocacy efforts, as they provide support, resources, and a platform for individuals and families to raise their concerns and seek help. You can become an advocate for your child, but your child can also learn to speak up for themselves (self-advocacy).

There is a clear benefit to seeking professional legal help. Legal experts can provide valuable insights, guide you through intricate legal processes, and ensure your case is presented effectively. However, their services can be expensive, making them unaffordable for some families. If you are on a low income or receiving certain types of benefits, you may be eligible for legal aid.

Some parents may opt to hire an advocate, who is not a lawyer. In England, advocacy work concerning SEN operates without specific regulations or strict rules for how it should be done. When seeking an advocate, it is imperative that you thoroughly assess their background and credentials. Verify their qualifications and professional experience and consider seeking insights from others who have used their services. It is essential to know how much they charge, whether or not they are easy to reach, and whether they have any liability insurance. There are helpful guidelines on finding an advocate published on the Council for Disabled Children's website – a link to which can be found in the "online resources" section at the end of this book.

It is possible to handle appeals and disability discrimination claims at the tribunal, as well as to make complaints about a school or LA, without a lawyer or an advocate. Many parents manage these processes without legal representation. Consider exploring the comprehensive resources available online, reaching out to helplines, and leveraging the support services provided by reputable organisations such as IPSEA, SOS!SEN and other charities.

Free assistance is available through your local Information, Advice and Support Service (known as IASS, or SENDIASS). SENDIASS stands for Special Educational Needs and Disabilities Information Advice and Support Service. This service is free and confidential; it offers information to families and young people dealing with SEN and disabilities. There is a SENDIASS in every LA in England.

You can locate your local SENDIASS by searching online. It provides advocacy services such as helping parents understand their rights, assisting with EHCPs, participating in meetings with parents, and ensuring the child's or young person's needs are appropriately addressed in the education system. Although funded by LAs, SENDIAS services are legally required to maintain independence from the LA and provide impartial information, advice and support.

Young people aged 16 and over

As mentioned earlier, legal rights granted under the CFA 2014 are automatically passed from parents to young people when the young people reach the end of compulsory schooling. Generally, this is at the age of 16.

There can be some confusion with the age of participation in education or training, which is 18 years under the Education and Skills Act 2008. Even after the young person turns 16, LAs continue to bear a broad duty to support and facilitate young people in engaging with education or training, and particularly to ensure that adequate provisions are made for those with EHCPs. Yet this requirement does not alter the definition of "compulsory school age".

Note that the CFA 2014 applies only to specific areas of decision-making. By way of example, once young people reach the end of compulsory school age, they gain rights such as the right to initiate EHC needs assessments or to lodge tribunal appeals. Matters such as living arrangements and personal finances are not included. In most cases, parents continue to play significant roles in supporting the young person's choices regarding their education and training.

At this point in life, young people begin to take the lead in deciding about their education. Also, they can become self-advocates. If they choose to do so, they learn to stand up for what they believe is right and to participate actively in decisions that affect their lives. Self-advocacy involves asserting one's own needs and preferences, whether it is in personal matters, school, work, or any other aspect of life.

It is important to consider how young people with SEN can exercise their rights effectively within the legal framework, taking into account any concerns that may arise regarding their mental capacity limitations. Section 80 of the CFA 2014 addresses this issue. It draws on the Mental Capacity Act 2005 to define what "lacking capacity" means.

The Mental Capacity Act 2005 applies to individuals aged 16 and above who live in England or Wales and who lack the capacity to make certain or all decisions for themselves. It establishes a legal framework to uphold and protect the process of decision-making.

Section 1 of the Mental Capacity Act 2005 outlines five crucial principles regarding decision-making on behalf of individuals who may lack capacity. These principles offer a clear framework to ensure that the best interests of the individual are upheld.

"The principles

1. *The following principles apply for the purposes of this Act.*

2. *A person must be assumed to have capacity unless it is established that he lacks capacity.*

3. *A person is not to be treated as unable to make a decision unless all practicable steps to help him to do so have been taken without success.*

4. *A person is not to be treated as unable to make a decision merely because he makes an unwise decision.*

5. *An act done, or decision made, under this Act for or on behalf of a person who lacks capacity must be done, or made, in his best interests.*

6. *Before the act is done, or the decision is made, regard must be had to whether the purpose for which it is needed can be as effectively achieved in a way that is less restrictive of the person's rights and freedom of action."*

In essence, according to the Mental Capacity Act 2005, a person is considered to lack capacity if – at the specific moment in question – they are unable to make a decision on their own regarding a particular matter, owing to an impairment or disturbance in the functioning of their mind or brain. Importantly, the absence of capacity cannot be determined based solely on a person's age, appearance, or any condition or behaviour that might lead others to form unwarranted assumptions about their capacity.

The key takeaway from this is that whether someone has or lacks capacity is not a fixed, permanent state. Capacity must be assessed each time a decision needs to be made with regard to that specific decision at hand. Within the SEND COP 2015, a person's capacity (or lack of it) is explicitly linked to their ability to make a specific decision precisely when that decision becomes necessary. Annex 1 of the SEND COP 2015 also provides valuable guidance and offers illustrative examples in this field.

Regulation 64 of the SEND Regulations 2014 introduces the concept of an "alternative person". When a young person lacks capacity under certain circumstances, references to the young person should also encompass the alternative person. The alternative person is typically the representative of that young person or, if the young person lacks such a representative, the alternative person defaults to their parent. This is known as "statutory substitution".

However, such substitution does not mean the young person is completely replaced by their parent or someone else in every situation. By way of example, the LA still has to take into account the young person's views, wishes and feelings, along with consideration of their parent's or representative's perspective.

Further reading

To stay informed about the latest updates and to gain valuable insights into navigating the world of SEN, I recommend subscribing to the Special Needs Jungle online newsletter. This invaluable resource provides timely information on changes in policies, as well as heartfelt stories from other families on similar journeys. These narratives can be a wellspring of inspiration and a source of practical strategies for advocacy.

It is also worth considering joining Facebook groups that are dedicated to SEN discussions. There are specific Facebook groups that correspond to nearly every LA in England. These groups are typically closed, reserved for parents, and are accessible only to those who live in the respective area.

These communities offer a supportive space where you can connect with others facing similar challenges and exchange invaluable advice. Becoming part of these networks will not only expand your knowledge, but also provide a community of individuals ready to offer guidance and support.

You can learn more about the Mental Capacity Act 2005 and its regime on the website of the charity Mind. The website link is in the "online resources" section at the end of this book.

Take a moment

Take a moment to write down your thoughts and ideas.

Among the questions to consider might be: how has this chapter expanded your perception of advocacy, especially in the context of SEN?

Consider the various roles of advocates, who might include parents, educators and self-advocates.

How do these roles contribute to the well-being and rights of children and young people with SEN?

PART 2: A how-to guide to the EHCP and how to keep it updated

Chapter 5:
Education sections (B, F, and I)

Introduction

The journey of learning how to develop an effective EHCP begins with a focus on Sections B, F, and I. These are commonly referred to as the education sections of the EHCP.

All the child's or young person's learning difficulties and disabilities should be documented in Section B. This section should reflect the education challenges that are pinpointed in reports from professionals.

Section F is where the SEP must be clearly outlined.

Section I in the final EHCP specifies the type of school that is determined appropriate, such as mainstream or special, primary or secondary, and so on. Typically, it also names a particular school – although exceptions apply.

'Picture this' exercise

The contents of education sections form a true cornerstone of the plan. It should not come as a surprise that they are interconnected.

Use a visualisation technique to create mental images while you read. This may help you to grasp and remember things better.

Imagine a sunny children's clinic with large windows that let in natural light. The walls are adorned with colourful, child-friendly art. A shelf with books and toys keeps young patients engaged. The receptionist greets them with a smile and offers stickers. It is an inviting space.

Once you enter the consulting room, you meet the doctor who is ready to see your child. **Section B**, much like the detailed notes taken by the doctor, is focused on recording and documenting all learning difficulties and disabilities. They are akin to symptoms, and the doctor can help best if they know all of them. In the EHCP, these detailed notes form Section B of the plan.

Next, picture the same doctor as they write a personalised treatment plan to address the specific needs of the patient. In the same way, in the EHCP, **Section F** specifies the SEP required and the plan should ensure that the specification aligns with the child's or young person's requirements.

Section I, in the same way the doctor prescribes the exact medicine, treatment or therapy that the patient needs, is focused on selecting the right school or institution. This section is there to ensure that the chosen educational setting fits with the child's or young person's needs and provides the best environment for their education journey.

All the actions described above happen in a particular order. Prescription does not come before diagnosis or preparation of the treatment plan. In the same way, Section B must be considered before Section F, and Section I should not influence the contents of Sections B or F. Adherence to the correct sequence ensures that an EHCP is logical and can be implemented effectively.

Take a moment to immerse yourself in this visualisation. How did the doctor's office feel? Was it welcoming or quite formal? People tend to view doctors as helpers and guides, which is a perspective deeply rooted in society's mindset. In this context, the metaphor can help you to piece together all the education sections to underline their interconnectedness and importance.

Section B: the child's or young person's SEN

Section B provides information on the child's or young person's SEN, which is identified in the expert reports listed in Section K. As you recall from Chapter 1, the term SEN refers to any special educational need that the child or young person has that calls for SEP.

Here are the content guidelines for Section B, in the form that they appear in the SEND COP 2015 (the table in Paragraph 9.69). This is what Section B is required to include.

- *"All of the child or young person's identified special educational needs must be specified.*
- *SEN may include needs for health and social care provision that are treated as special educational provision because they educate or train the child or young person (see paragraphs 9.73 [of the SEND COP 2015] onwards)."*

The EHCP does not have a fixed format and there are various templates provided by LAs. These EHCP templates could be easily found online using platforms such as Google or any other search engine. However, it is important to note that many of these templates come up with their own potential challenges. For this reason, I have not included any of them as examples in this book. Now, let's take a closer look at some scenarios that commonly come up in these templates.

Sections are in a confusing order

There is more than one Section B and several sections are combined (for example, B, E, and F) without clear differentiation of their content. All the child's or young person's needs should be clearly identified in Section B. Yet sometimes this information is scattered across different parts of the plan or mixed in with descriptions of outcomes and/or SEP. This can lead to potential issues, such as:

- the LA may misjudge the child's/young person's learning difficulties and/or disabilities;
- the LA may overlook some of the child's or young person's learning difficulties and/or disabilities; and

■ all of the above may affect the levels or types of SEP that are specified in Section F, as well as the choice of the education placement in Section I.

You can highlight such issues to the LA and request corrections to any unclear or confusing material.

Summary section

It is helpful to have a plain and succinct summary in Section B of the plan. This can expedite the reader's understanding of the broader context, especially as the subsequent content in this section is usually presented in bullet-point form. The purpose of this summary is to provide a comprehensive understanding of the child or young person. This is especially important for readers such as supply teachers, who may have no prior knowledge of the child's or young person's needs and may have to review the plan quickly. This helps to ensure that all readers, regardless of their familiarity with the plan, know what to expect.

Place in which to detail the diagnosis

Some templates include a separate section in which one can state just the child's or young person's diagnosis. This serves as a convenient reference point because it enables readers to locate and grasp this information easily. Although there may be arguments from the LA that the diagnosis should not be specified in this section owing to its broad nature, most education professionals are familiar with diagnostic terms. They find it helpful to know which diagnoses have been associated with the child or young person as an initial reference. The descriptions of needs in Section B provide a deeper understanding of how this child or young person is specifically affected by their diagnosis and offer insights for those working with them.

Parents may frequently face the challenge of not having a formal diagnosis, especially in the context of neurodevelopmental conditions. By way of example, securing an autism diagnosis can be a lengthy and complex process, even when clear traits are evident. Section B proves valuable (particularly where the formal diagnosis is pending), as it documents the manifestations of a condition. As shown in SG v Denbighshire CC [2018] UKUT 369 (AAC), what really matters is how the difficulty or disability affects a person, not the specific medical reasons behind it. So, you do not need to know why exactly someone has SEN to get the help and support they need.

Place to note down strengths

Many LAs allocate separate spaces in which to detail strengths and many templates require such descriptions. This practice does not align with the guidance in Paragraph 9.69 of the SEND COP 2015 regarding Section B content. Paragraph 9.69 emphasises that all identified SEN should be specified and that Section B does not require the inclusion of strengths. But Paragraph 9.61 of the SEND COP 2015 contains a rationale for including descriptions of such strengths. This paragraph highlights the importance of positively showcasing the child's or young person's abilities and accomplishments within EHCPs. The exact location for this information is not explicitly defined. It could be argued that strengths might be better placed in Section A, but due to the Section A's limited enforcement power, the preference is often made for them to be recorded in Section B instead. It is vital to approach the drafting process thoughtfully, to consider the potential impact of information and to ensure that the conveyed meaning is accurate and not misleading. Please refer to the example below.

Areas of need – headings

Learning difficulties are typically categorised under headings such as communication and interaction, cognition and learning, social, emotional, and mental health, and sensory and/or physical needs. These headings are derived from Paragraph 5.32 of the SEND COP 2015 and can serve as a helpful checklist to ensure that everything is covered. For older children and young people, there should be a part on preparation for adulthood. You might want to revisit the discussion of these areas of need (see pp.45-49). These broad areas serve as an overview that can guide on the range of needs that should be considered in Section B. The goal is not to fit a child into a specific category but to determine the appropriate actions that the school must take. In reality, many children have needs that overlap across these areas, and their needs may change over time.

Health and care needs

Section B also encompasses health and social care needs that require provision that educates or trains. The focus here is on addressing factors that influence a child's or young person's ability to participate effectively in the classroom and to learn. For instance, needs for services such as speech and language therapy are included to emphasise the crucial role of communication in education.

Provision such as physiotherapy may be incorporated to alleviate musculoskeletal issues that hinder learning due to pain. Anxiety, which significantly impacts a child's or young person's learning capacity, should also be considered. Also, physical concerns such as incontinence can affect the child's education and training, particularly when discomfort disrupts their education experience.

When reviewing Section B, it is practical to focus on difficulties rather than "needs" in their everyday meaning, because thinking this way makes it easier to understand and address the child's or young person's requirements. People often mix up SEN with SEP in this section, as they try to identify what their child logically needs (SEP) rather than what they struggle with (SEN). Describing special needs in terms of difficulties helps to pinpoint the specific areas in which children or young people may face challenges or barriers.

The following is an example of how wording that relates to difficulties can be used in Section B.

Avoid using:

"Jack needs regular practice to strengthen his hands and fingers, due to hypermobility, in order to support efficient handwriting and pencil grip."

Consider using:

"Jack experiences difficulties with his hands and fingers due to hypermobility, which affects his ability to write and hold a pencil efficiently."

The second sentence clearly describes the specific difficulties related to the child's hypermobility. It focuses on the challenges Jack faces with his hands and fingers and provides a clear understanding of the barriers he encounters. In contrast, the first sentence jumps directly to the provision required, which is more appropriately included in Section F of the EHCP.

As the above example shows, it is important to distinguish between content appropriate for Section B and that appropriate for Section F of the EHCP to avoid any confusion. In Section B, each aspect of the child's or young person's learning difficulties and disabilities should be addressed separately, as each will require a distinct SEP that should be outlined in Section F.

When discussing strengths, context is key. It is important to keep in mind that the child or young person is often compared with another child or young person and that a broader understanding of the situation is required.

In other words, to ensure accuracy, establish a well-defined point of comparison. When the child is compared with peers, specify the reference standard or methodology (such as, for example, national curriculum levels) to ensure transparency. In addition, when various aspects of the child's or young person's abilities are assessed, strengths and difficulties should be connected to provide a complete picture.

Review the following example of how a strength is described in Section B.

Avoid using:

Jane's receptive language is within average range.

Consider using:

Jane's average range of receptive language skills supports her learning by allowing her to understand and follow two-step instructions given by teachers, as well as to comprehend academic content in the classroom that is appropriate for her age level.

The term "within average range" – as used in the first sentence to describe language ability – lacks specificity in terms of the aspects being assessed, such as social language or comprehension of instructions. Assessments cover various language elements, and reliance on averages alone can be misleading.

A child may excel in certain areas but face challenges in expressing themselves or understanding language in different contexts. This presents a "spiky profile" of abilities (an uneven pattern of skill-related strengths and weaknesses).

The vague characterisation of "within average range" does not provide meaningful insight into a child's or young person's language abilities.

When too much focus is placed on strengths and there is no proper context, it is possible to unintentionally overlook the underlying needs and to create a misleading impression of what the child or young person truly requires. This can give the incorrect impression that they do not need much support, which may undermine the importance of having appropriate help.

When drafting strengths, link them to how they support the child's learning. This is important to maintain a balanced perspective so that the document addresses the genuine needs effectively.

Some people question whether giftedness or exceptional ability falls under the category of SEN. Gifted children may encounter challenges in traditional educational settings due to a lack of sufficient stimulation, which results in them feeling bored or frustrated. The case of *S v Special Educational Needs Tribunal [2005] EWHC 196 (Admin)* explored the idea that these children might meet the requirement of having a "significantly greater difficulty in learning" compared with their peers. The decision clarified that exceptional ability alone did not qualify as a learning difficulty.

Section F: SEP required by the child or young person

Here are the content guidelines for Section F, as they are written in the SEND COP 2015 (the table in Paragraph 9.69). Section F is required to include the following.

- "Provision must be detailed and specific and should normally be quantified, for example, in terms of the type, hours and frequency of support and level of expertise, including where this support is secured through a personal budget.

- Provision must be specified for each and every need specified in Section B. It should be clear how the provision will support achievement of the outcomes.

- Where health or social care provision educates or trains a child or young person, it must appear in this section (see Paragraph 9.73 [of the SEND COP 2015]).

- There should be clarity as to how advice and information gathered has informed the provision specified. Where the local authority has departed from that advice, they should say so and give reasons for it.

- In some cases, flexibility will be required to meet the changing needs of the child or young person, including flexibility in the use of a personal budget.

- The plan should specify:

  - any appropriate facilities and equipment, staffing arrangements and curriculum;

  - any appropriate modifications to the application of the National Curriculum, where relevant;

  - any appropriate exclusions from the application of the National Curriculum or the course being studied in a post-16 setting, in detail, and the provision which it is proposed to substitute for any such exclusions in order to maintain a balanced and broadly based curriculum;

  - where residential accommodation is appropriate, that fact; and

> ■ where there is a personal budget, the outcomes to which it is
> intended to contribute (detail of the arrangements for a personal
> budget, including any direct payment, must be included in the plan
> and these should be set out in section J)
>
> ■ See Paragraph 9.131 [of the SEND COP 2015] onwards for details
> of duties on the local authority to maintain the special educational
> provision in the EHC plan."

Over time, tribunals have extensively examined what Section F can include. As the title suggests, its purpose is to record all the SEP that the child or young person needs. The term SEP refers to extra education support that goes beyond what mainstream nurseries, schools or colleges in England normally provide for children aged two or older. For children under the age of two, it refers to any education support they may need.

It is important to understand that there is no need to check every single school in England to see what they offer. The responsibility falls on the LA or a tribunal to use its professional judgement to determine what is considered a typical provision for kids of a certain age group. Once they have that typical provision in mind, they can decide whether the education support needed by a particular child or young person goes beyond what is generally provided. If it does, then it falls under the category of SEP.

To help illustrate this, here is an example from the case of *EAM v East Sussex CC [2022] UKUT 193 (AAC)*. This case involved a girl who had a condition called electromagnetic hypersensitivity. Although there is a perception that electromagnetic hypersensitivity is not scientifically valid, this decision has practical implications because it establishes a broad understanding of what qualifies as SEP.

The girl involved in the case could not use computers with Wi-Fi at school because the Wi-Fi caused difficulties for her. Even though she did not have intellectual impairments, her inability to use the school's facilities caused her to be considered disabled. Initially, the school tried to accommodate her needs by maintaining a wired connection for the school computers. Unfortunately, the situation took a turn when new management took over and decided to introduce Wi-Fi instead, which made it impossible for her to attend the school. Her family did a lot of research and sought advice on how she could be supported at school.

Electromagnetic hypersensitivity is a condition that causes people to experience physical symptoms when they are exposed to non-ionising radiation or devices that use or produce it, such as Wi-Fi, mobile phones, and Bluetooth. The child in this example faced difficulties because she had to rely on computer programs to communicate rather than talking directly to her teachers. She also had sensory issues that made it hard for her to use electronic devices.

In this case, the Upper Tribunal decided that the creation of a learning environment that did not include Wi-Fi could be considered SEP. This decision was based on the fact that the difficulty was associated with education and the equipment she required surpassed what was typically available in schools across England. The reasoning in this case aligns with many other previous decisions. In cases where a child needs specific learning conditions (eg, small classes), these are considered SEP. Other examples of SEP can be found on pp.49-52.

Appreciating the distinction between "education and training provision" and "provision that educates or trains" is also crucial. This matters in cases in which the provision is also health or social care provision. If a provision that is related to healthcare or social care helps to educate or train a child or young person, it is considered SEP and should be included in Section F.

To illustrate this point, consider the insights shared by the Upper Tribunal in *DC and DC v Hertfordshire CC [2016] UKUT 379 (AAC)*. In this case, a few examples were provided for comparison. In the first example, a student with an anxiety disorder received mindfulness training. The objective was to help the student to remain calm, stay focused in class, and interact effectively with peers.

In the second example, the same student also received cognitive behavioural therapy to help them acquire skills to manage sudden episodes of anxiety.

In the third example, the student underwent regular hypnosis sessions as a means to address and prevent self-harming behaviours.

In the first two examples, the interventions involved structured training. This training was focused on the acquisition of coping strategies that supported the student's education experience within the classroom and their social integration with peers. Therefore, these interventions could be considered educational in nature.

However, in the third example, the focus was on modifying the student's behaviour through subconscious practices. This type of intervention was not deemed education provision, as it was more akin to taking an antibiotic for a sore throat. Hence, the provision in the first two examples was found to align with Section F, whereas the third example would be more appropriate in Section G as a health provision.

It is crucial to ensure that the provisions included in Section F are specific and detailed. High-quality descriptions enable teachers, assistants and others involved in the child's education to understand how to provide the necessary support. However, achieving this is not always straightforward.

The overview of the law on specificity and quantification can be found in the case of *Worcestershire County Council v SE [2020] UKUT 217 (AAC)*, particularly in Paragraph 74, in which Judge West's explanation is recorded. The case of *London Borough of Redbridge v HO (SEN) [2020] UKUT 323 (AAC)* introduced additional principles that are outlined in Judge Lane's words in Paragraph 21.

These overviews within case law and the range of principles discussed in them highlight the highly debated nature of this topic. They serve as useful starting points from which to understand Section F. A summary of these principles is given below. They can assist as an initial guide to help you to analyse Section F in your plan.

■ The EHCP is a standalone legal document that sets out the LA's duties. It must clearly outline the LA's obligations and provide a comprehensive understanding of the required SEP.

■ The key question for any plan is whether it is clear and specific enough to eliminate any doubt about what has been deemed necessary for the individual case.

- The focus should be on the unique circumstances of each case. A more detailed case may require more specific provisions. There is no need, however, to include every last detail.

- The plan should not only cater to the current situation but also account for the future. It is not appropriate to constantly revise a plan in order to achieve absolute precision. Professionals must have adequate freedom to exercise their judgement based on the circumstances at hand.

- If specific levels of support are not specified beyond a certain date, the support may lack the necessary level of specificity.

- Specifying a certain number of hours per week is usually necessary, but it is not a prerequisite for the plan to be legal.

- It is not appropriate for Section F to state that an "assessment" is required. An assessment is not considered a provision in of itself but, rather, a tool used to determine the necessary provision.

- Recommendations rather than requirements – as well as wording such as "opportunities" or "tailored programmes" – should be avoided, as they may lack the required specificity. It is unlikely that vague terms such as "support", "input", "interventions" and "opportunities" will be sufficient to explain the provision required if there are no specific details.

- In some cases, flexibility should be retained, potentially to a significant degree. However, retention of flexibility should not be used as an excuse to omit specificity in cases in which it is reasonable to provide detailed information. Quantification may not be necessary if flexibility is in the best interest of the child.

- If the child is to be educated in a mainstream rather than a special school, there may be a need for greater specificity in Section F.

Understandably, the sheer number of rules may be overwhelming. If you encounter a particularly complex issue, it is always a good idea to seek professional legal advice. The information provided above serves as a reminder that the rules governing SEP are not always straightforward and there may be alternative options to consider.

To simplify the process of outlining provisions in Section F of an EHCP, a practical approach that many people recommend is the use of the **"who, what, when and how long"** writing formula (it comes from the case of *EC v North East Lincolnshire LA [205] UKUT 0648 (AAC)*). Application of this formula helps to achieve clarity and thoroughness in descriptions of SEP.

In this context, the **"who"** refers to the person or entity responsible for the delivery of the specified provision and should be identified. The **"what"** highlights the specific details and nature of the provision. The **"when"** specifies the timing or frequency of the provision. Lastly, the **"how long"** addresses the duration of the provision; this could be the length of each session, the overall duration of the support, and/or any other relevant timeframe. By using this method, you can ensure that the SEP outlined in Section F is sufficiently specific and detailed.

Troubleshooting strategies and practical solutions for writing Section F

There are examples below of what actions to take and what pitfalls to avoid.

Wording that is unclear or uses vague language

It is often observed by the users of EHCPs that Section F contains vague terminology. The term "weasel words" is often used to describe the vague language in Section F, while the unspecific provision is often referred to as "woolly".

Imagine a "weasel word" as a sneaky little phrase that is designed to sound important and specific but leaves you scratching your head because it is so vague and unclear. Using weasel words helps people to avoid saying something definite in their statements. It allows them to deny a specific meaning later if questioned.

"Sneaky weasel"   *"Woolly sheep"*

It is important to identify weasel words in the EHCP, because unclear wording makes it difficult to action SEP in Section F.

Table 4 below gives some example weasel words that you can refer to every time you review Section F.

Table 4: Examples of vague terms ("weasel words") that have been used in Section F

Opportunities for	Will benefit from	Access to
Up to	Regular support	Periodic
To be determined	As required	May be helpful
If available	Adult	No more than
Small groups	Might or may	One-to-one support

When reviewing an EHCP, closely examine any vague terms and consider whether they add useful definitions or create uncertainty. Unclear or vague wording in the plan may result in the SEP not being delivered in the correct quantity, by the appropriate person, or even at all.

It may be necessary to remove such terms or to introduce more specific words and details to ensure clarity about the intended delivery of provision and to avoid potential difficulties later on.

Case law has established that the provision in Section F should be "so specific and so clear as to leave no room for doubt as to what has been decided and what is needed in the individual case" (this is a quote from *L v Clarke & Somerset CC [1998] ELR 129*). If you identify any vague or ambiguous language in the draft EHCP prepared by the LA, you can highlight to them that such wording may be in breach of the legal requirements. If the unclear wording comes from an expert report, the LA may need to seek further clarification and advice from the professionals who authored the report.

Let's consider the following examples of vague wording that might come up in Section F.

> Jyoti will be provided with opportunities for social interaction and inclusion within the school environment.

Although the phrase "opportunities for" may sound promising and full of potential, its inclusion in the plan does not guarantee the actual provision of services or support for the child or young person. The case of *B-M and B-M v Oxfordshire CC (SEN) [2018] UKUT 35 (AAC)* clarified that terms like "opportunities for" were vague, meaningless and unenforceable.

> James will be provided with access to appropriate learning resources and materials.

The use of the term "access to" may give the impression of privilege, inclusivity or availability of resources. However, similar to the term "opportunities for", it lacks clarity and precision. For some children, mere access to or opportunities for something may not be sufficient to meet their specific needs. It is necessary to go beyond general statements and to provide clear and targeted descriptions that address the requirements of a child or young person.

> Yousuf will be provided with regular sensory breaks.

Terms such as "regular", "periodic" or "frequent" are vague and unhelpful when the EHCP user tries to quantify the provision required. In the phrase "regular sensory breaks", it is critical to define what "regular" means. Is it a quick break every hour or a longer break every few hours? Be as specific as possible to avoid any misunderstandings.

> Nikita will benefit from additional support in the classroom.

The term "benefit from" carries various interpretations. However, the LA must set up provision that directly targets Nikita's specific needs. The choices and decisions regarding his support should not be delegated in the future to individuals who are not qualified to decide what is needed. To ensure clarity and to maximise the education outcomes for Nikita, replace the vague expression "will benefit from" with a precise specification of the support he requires.

> Sarah will receive up to three hours of additional support per week from the Therapy Assistant.

The use of the phrase "up to" introduces an element of uncertainty, akin to a game of chance in which the outcome may vary significantly. It implies that either no specific requirement is necessary or that the determination of the amount is left to the discretion of an undisclosed decision-maker. To avoid leaving Sarah in a state of uncertainty, specific details regarding the quantity of support she requires should be included. The inclusion of specific and detailed recommendations, such as "five times a week for 30 minutes each time", will ensure that Sarah's academic progress is on the right track.

Therapies can be delivered either directly or indirectly. Direct therapy is that conducted by an actual therapist, such as a speech and language professional, directly with the child or young person. On the other hand, indirect therapy is usually carried out by a trained teaching assistant. It is important to specify in the plan whether the therapy is direct or indirect. This information helps to determine the amount of time that the child or young person will spend with a specialist and what responsibilities fall on the school staff.

> Ayodele will receive support from adults.

In order to provide clarity and ensure that Ayodele receives appropriate support, it is crucial to specify the roles and responsibilities of the individuals referred to as "adults". This will help to identify the education professionals, support staff, or other designated individuals who possess the necessary expertise to meet Ayodele's needs effectively.

> Lara will have one-to-one support during whole class phonic teaching sessions.

It is vital that the plan clearly designates that one-to-one support will be dedicated specifically to the child, rather than be spread across other pupils, as this can lead to problems and potential lack of support. Additionally, the assumption that the class teacher or general school staff will provide all support is inappropriate and fails to acknowledge the child's or young person's unique needs. Avoid assumptions that any support staff, such as playground support assistants or cleaners, can fulfil specialised roles.

Wording that permits changes without proper process

The wording in Section F should not provide for unilateral amendment of provision by the LA or any third party. Any change to an EHCP should be made only after completion of a proper process (eg, an annual review) so that the parents or young person (as appropriate) have a right to appeal.

Below is an example of wording that should be questioned:

> The provision initially includes three individual speech therapy sessions per term for three terms. Following this period, the therapist will assess and evaluate the need for continuation, potential adjustments (increasing or reducing sessions), or discontinuation.

The practice specified here is not permitted because it allows changes in support without any process of amendment, so parents are deprived of a chance to appeal. The wording suggests that provision can be altered without any challenge, which could result in the abrupt discontinuation of speech therapy without any recourse. Case law, such as *E v Rotherham MBC [2002] ELR 266, [2001] EWHC Admin 432*, has determined such practices to be unlawful. Question and challenge such wording to ensure that EHCPs align with the law and protect the rights of children and young people.

Wording related to use of programmes

It is important to be cautious if an EHCP includes references to programmes. The relevant provision in the EHCP lacks value if the content of such programmes is not specified.

Here are two examples of wording that should be questioned.

> "[C] requires a programme to develop his social communication and social interaction skills delivered in one-to-one and small group settings with opportunities to practice (sic) new skills learnt throughout the day."
>
> "[C] requires a structured programme to develop his motor planning co-ordination skills."

The above wordings are taken from the case of *B-M and B-M v Oxfordshire CC (SEN) [2018] UKUT 35 (AAC)*. They were found to be unlawful. The problem here is that the provision for tailored programmes lacks substance and does not provide any meaningful information. Although the purpose of the required programme is described, its content is not specified at all.

To be more specific, EHCPs may refer to established programmes such as "Zones of Regulation" or "Visualising and Verbalising". To ensure clarity and accountability, Section F should include information about who will be responsible for setting up the programme, who will deliver it, their required training and supervision and the frequency of the sessions.

The EHCP may also include information about arrangements for additional training. By way of example, this could involve a teaching assistant who participates in individual therapy sessions with the child.

Documentation of these specifics can help to regulate and monitor the programme effectively.

Wording that incorporates flexibility

Paragraph 9.69 of the SEND COP 2015 states that flexibility may be required in some cases to address a child's or young person's changing needs. The case of *IPSEA v Secretary of State (2003) EWCA Civ 07 (2003) ELR 86* established an important principle in this regard. The needs may change as the child or young person grows or due to their interaction with the environment, and these expected changes may justify the use of less specificity in Section F. However, it is not acceptable to leave the provision unspecified or not quantified simply to meet the needs of the system (for example, the school or the LA).

In all cases, flexibility should not be seen as an excuse to leave out specifics when detailed information could reasonably be provided. If changes to the provision are required, it is far better to discuss them during the annual review process to address any potential amendments. If this is done, the necessity for built-in flexibility can be eliminated, which will ensure that the plan contains a more comprehensive and tailored approach to the child's or young person's needs.

The following example demonstrates the concept of flexibility, taken from the case of *SB v Herefordshire County Council [2018] UKUT 141 (AAC)*. One of the issues, in this case, revolved around the language used in the EHCP, which stated that the child (a girl named Jessica) required instruction in "small class groups". The question here was whether the inherent flexibility in this wording was justifiable.

In this quite complex example, the court considered the entire EHCP, including both the desired outcome in Section E and the SEP in Section F. This case shows that sometimes the provisions in an EHCP must be reviewed together. The overall interpretation in this case suggested that the court aimed to create an education plan for a child who required significant education support, particularly in areas such as literacy.

The provision for Jessica to be taught in small groups related to the following outcome in her plan.

"[Jessica] has functional learning skills in literacy and numeracy and can apply these in context."

The specified provision included the following.

"Staff need to have an appropriate level of expertise in language and communication needs and there should be an emphasis upon the development of [Jessica's] self-esteem..."

"[Jessica] needs an environment where staff can support her understanding of language. [Jessica] needs to be supported to use active listening strategies."

"[Jessica] needs to be educated by staff who are familiar in educating young people with expressive language difficulties, aware of her historic language difficulties and who are able to provide support for her word finding difficulties."

"[Jessica] must be shown and taught the following skills..." (The skills were learning to identify common number blends and their usual pronunciation, as well as identifying the 'magic e', and being taught or frequently shown consonants that are sometimes hard and sometimes soft).

"Information should be broken down into chunks and explained in different ways with feedback provided on each task to check her understanding."

"A numeracy programme which uses a structured approach allowing for repetition and over learning."

"[Jessica] requires support in the classroom to ensure her understanding and expressive use of relevant vocabulary in the learning context."

Separately, the plan also included the following provision.

> *"[Jessica] to be provided with access to a Teaching Assistant for 24 hours each week so that she is enabled to receive the programme detailed above [in the plan] individually or in small groups with peers of similar ability."*
>
> *"Provide [Jessica] with sufficient time to think and process information."*
>
> *"Staff to monitor for signs of falling confidence and self-esteem and to take action if this occurs."*

It was determined that the exact size of the small groups in which Jessica would be taught did not have to be specified to achieve the desired outcome. The decision was based on the understanding that the appropriate size of the small groups could vary without compromising Jessica's education.

This determination took into account various factors. These included Jessica's education profile and her diverse support requirements across different subjects, the uncertainty surrounding the development of her confidence and self-esteem, and the necessity for her to learn alongside peers of similar abilities whose numbers could not be predicted accurately.

These findings showed that it could be acceptable to be flexible when giving education in small groups. While the EHCP did not specify an upper limit to the size of the groups, it was evident that the group size was to be small enough to deliver effectively the provision outlined in the plan.

Jessica's case shows that in some situations it is difficult to be specific and a little flexibility might be necessary. However, that flexibility should only be used when it helps the child and not for other reasons. In case of any confusion or disagreement, it is always important to consider what is best for the child or young person, and to make decisions based on that.

Case law recognises that special schools have the expertise to meet children's needs and can adapt quickly as they develop, so less specification and detail may be required in descriptions of the support to be given to these children. There is an example of this in the judgement of *East Sussex CC v TW [2016] UKUT 528 (AAC)*. The principle that special schools have the expertise to meet SEN and to respond flexibly as the needs change may not apply as strongly to generic types of special schools. By way of example, those described as catering for unspecified "moderate learning difficulties". In such schools, staff may not have expertise in all areas of learning difficulties, making flexibility in responding to changing needs less assured. Additionally, special schools may benefit from the inclusion of details in Section F regarding provision to demonstrate the child's need for specialist support and potentially to secure additional funding. Overall, the provision of reasonably detailed description – especially in specialist areas of support offered by the school – is generally in the best interest of the child or young person, particularly to avoid potential disputes in case of school transfers.

Wording related to "education otherwise than at a setting" (EOTAS)

If a child receives education or tuition at home or in a non-school environment, the details should be clearly stated in Section F. Such information should not be placed in Section I, which is specifically for placement information.

When a child receives EOTAS, it may be necessary to provide more specific information in the EHCP. In the case of *DM v Cornwall County Council [2022] UKUT 230 (AAC)*, the Upper Tribunal considered that education provision within a school setting could be assumed to some extent, while the provision of EOTAS may need to be explicitly stated. The level of specificity required in an EHCP will always depend on the unique circumstances of the child's or young person's case.

Wording related to funding arrangements

Different wording related to funding formulas or banding arrangements is used in Section F. However, according to Regulation 12 of the SEND Regulations 2014, the provision of specific information about funding or funding sources is not required in the EHCP. The provision outlined in the plan should be delivered regardless of whether it exceeds the specified funding level. While it may be acceptable to include such wording, caution should be exercised to ensure that such wording does not mislead schools or families.

Here are some examples of wording that is related to funding arrangements and that might come up in EHCPs.

> *In accordance with the local authority's banding system and the provisions outlined in the SEN policy, Peter will have support at Band X.*

Here, an EHCP mentions the level of support a child will receive according to the LA's banding system. The issue with this approach is that reliance solely on banding arrangements can allow the LA to modify support without formally amending the EHCP, which is not fair to the child or young person. Instead, support should be described based on the actual needs, rather than just the allocated funds. The child or young person has the right to receive the help they require, regardless of its cost.

In simple terms, an LA can mention funding "bands" as a reference but this wording should not replace or limit the clear specification of the support needed. Make sure the necessary SEP is properly specified and provided without any compromises or changes.

> *This resource will require three hours of monthly support, with the local authority providing resourced provision funding to the school to be used in conjunction with the school's delegated funding.*

If the EHCP states that the school (or sometimes the NHS) will be responsible for providing support, remember that the responsibility for delivery of that support remains with the LA, even if it has delegated funds elsewhere for supporting SEN. Once stated in Section F, it becomes the duty of the LA to ensure that SEP is secured and provided. If there is a failure to deliver the specified SEP, the responsibility falls back on the LA. In cases in which delegated institutions are unable to secure the required provision with the allocated funds, the LA is obliged by law to step in and provide it. In a practical sense, it would be helpful to have a statement added in the above wording to the effect that the LA retains overall responsibility for ensuring that the SEP outlined in the plan is delivered. If there is resistance to this, cite Section 42(2) of the CFA 2014 ("the local authority must secure the specified special educational provision for the child or young person") to reinforce your position.

> *"In a mainstream school, the educational setting will receive a sum of £11,500, which will be used to deliver the provision as set out in Section F."*

Here, a mainstream school is supposed to be allocated a stated sum of money to deliver the SEP stated in Section F. Some families may worry whether the specified amount will be sufficient. As explained above, the inclusion of funding details in Section F is optional and not necessary. It is reassuring to know that it is the LA's responsibility to ensure adequate funding, regardless of the amount specified. Internal budgeting arrangements mentioned in this example can be challenged and the LA remains responsible for the provision of the required SEP, even if funding is reduced.

Here are some more tips:

- Consider including in the EHCP any additional time required for outside support professionals (such as specialist teachers and therapists) to prepare reports, contribute to plans and attend meetings, especially annual review meetings. This is important, unless there is already an agreement between the LA and the provider that covers these time requirements.

- EHCPs should align the provision with the child's or young person's needs, rather than the other way around. It is quite common for NHS therapy departments to suggest a standard provision for all children or young people, regardless of their specific difficulties. Ask your LA not to accept this approach and, if the NHS is unable to provide the required support, instead to instruct independent experts to recommend the appropriate provision that the child or young person truly requires.

- When reviewing Section F, make sure it reflects accurately the information provided in the experts' reports. Sometimes, important provisions are left out because they are costly or their inclusion may result in more expensive school placements. Ensure that all necessary support is included, regardless of the potential costs involved.

- LAs are not permitted to customise Section F to match only the provision available in the school they propose to name. Section F should include the support that the child or young person needs. If the chosen school cannot provide that support, the LA should either arrange for the necessary support to be funded at that school or consider naming a different school that can meet the child's or young person's needs.

- When parents have a specific school in mind, the SEP listed in Section F must align with what that school can offer and the LA needs to agree with it. It is important to be honest and to follow the proper process. Identify the provision that the child or young person genuinely needs, then explore the options with the available schools, including your preferred choice.

Section I: the name and type of the school, maintained nursery school, post-16 institution or other institution to be attended by the child or young person and the type of that institution

Here are the content guidelines for Section I, as included in the SEND COP 2015 (the table in Paragraph 9.69). This is what Section I is required to include.

- "The name and type of the school, maintained nursery school, post-16 institution or other institution to be attended by the child or young person and the type of that institution (or, where the name of a school or other institution is not specified in the EHC plan, the type of school or other institution to be attended by the child or young person).

- *These details must be included only in the final EHCP, not the draft EHCP sent to the child's parent or to the young person.*

- *See Paragraph 9.78 [of the SEND COP 2015] onwards for more details."*

The only permissible contents of Section I are the name and type of the education establishment that the child or young person will attend.

The LA is required to provide the draft EHCP, along with the appendices that contain the advice and information on which the contents are based, to the child's parent or the young person. When the LA sends the draft plan to the child's parents or to the young person, it should inform the parent or young person that they can ask for a specific school or institution to be named in the plan.

The draft plan should not already contain the name or type of the school or institution (Section 38(5) of the CFA 2014). This is because the LA should not pre-determine a specific school or type of school during the drafting of the plan. Instead, the plan should be tailored to the child's or young person's needs and should outline the provision that is necessary for them to meet their goals.

Now, let's explore the components/elements of Section I and what they can include.

Placement name

Unless compelled by Section 39 of the CFA 2014, the LA is not strictly obliged to name a specific school or institution in Section I. In practice, however, naming is common when specifying a "mainstream" type of school.

When a child or young person has an EHCP, the typical admission procedures for other children in the LA do not apply to them. The EHCP determines their placement.

There is a requirement that Section I of the draft EHCP be left blank so that the parents and young people can submit their preference. The LA may guide parents and young people on available schools and colleges when issuing a draft plan, although the ultimate choice lies with the parents or young person.

In cases where parents or the young person prefer a school or other institution outlined in Section 38(3) of the CFA 2014, they can make a request for it to the LA. Here is the list for your reference.

> "Section 38(3)
>
> (3) A school or other institution is within this subsection if it is:
>
> a. a maintained school
>
> b. a maintained nursery school
>
> c. an Academy
>
> d. an institution within the further education sector in England
>
> e. a non-maintained special school
>
> f. an institution approved by the Secretary of State under section 41 (independent special schools and special post-16 institutions: approval)."

This list covers a broad range of settings. The only schools or institutions not included are those that are entirely independent, so they are neither non-maintained, nor approved by the Secretary of State under Section 41, nor institutions within the further education sector. You can use the "Get Information About Schools" service on the gov.uk website to search for a specific school, which will indicate whether an independent placement is approved under Section 41.

Any school or institution that is named in Section I of the EHCP, unless wholly independent, is required by law to admit the child or young person.

Upon receiving a request for a specific placement, the LA must consult with the governing body of the school or institution. The LA must ensure that the EHCP identifies the requested school or institution, unless one of the conditions in Section 39(4) of the CFA 2014 is applicable, as follows.

"Section 39(4)

(4) This subsection applies where:

a. the school or other institution requested is unsuitable for the age, ability, aptitude or special educational needs of the child or young person concerned, or

b. the attendance of the child or young person at the requested school or other institution would be incompatible with:

i. the provision of efficient education for others, or

ii. the efficient use of resources."

It is essential to recognise that these are the only exceptions upon which the LA can rely to refuse the placement request, and no other factors can be considered.

The first exception applies if the chosen placement does not suit the child's or young person's age, ability, aptitude, or SEN. It is fairly straightforward – if the place cannot meet the needs or is not a good fit for the individual's learning style and special needs, it becomes a problem.

The second exception arises when the child's or young person's attendance would disrupt the provision of efficient education for others in that school. This commonly occurs in situations where the school is full or has reached or even exceeded its capacity. Adding another child or young person could negatively impact those already in the school.

The third exception comes into play when the child's or young person's attendance does not align with the efficient use of resources. In simple terms, if the chosen place is more expensive than what the LA suggests, it might not work. Please be mindful that there is a lot of case law on how this exception is applied.

If the school preferred by parents or young person differs from that selected by the LA, and both are suitable, there is another option. The family can offer to cover associated transport costs for the child or young person to attend their chosen school in order to reduce the burden on public funds. Then, in Section I, both placements can be named – with the condition that the family agrees to cover the transport costs to the preferred school where the child or young person will attend. This was looked at in the case of *Dudley MBC v Shurvinton [2012] EWCA Civ 346*.

Overall, this is a complex area, and an extensive body of case law has examined the application of the conditions mentioned above. To understand better the placement selection process, a valuable resource is the annually published *Noddy No-Nonsense Guide to SEN Law*, released by Matrix and Landmark Chambers. You can find the website links in the "online resources" section at the end of this book.

Placement type

Section I of the EHCP must contain details about the "type of school" that is deemed appropriate for the child or young person. The "type" of school mentioned in the EHCP usually refers to the different categories of schools, such as mainstream, special, or independent schools. This includes whether it is a nursery, primary or secondary school, and whether it is boarding or residential.

It is becoming common to see plans that detail the specific type of special school needed, such as a school for pupils with autism or a school for children with specific learning and language-based difficulties.

There are, however, certain situations that fall into a grey area. In these cases, it is important to determine whether a specific arrangement qualifies as a "school" or an "institution".

The legislation does not provide a specific definition for the term "school". Instead, its interpretation is determined on a case-by-case basis by the tribunal as a matter of fact. Likewise, the term "institution" is not defined in the legislation and, unfortunately, limited attention has been given to its interpretation in case law.

Certain scenarios can be ambiguous and, in such cases, it must be established whether a particular arrangement meets the criteria of a "school" or an "institution". To gain a better understanding of this issue, below is an exploration of two examples of different outcomes.

> *"[AB] will attend the GROW Project, a unit based at WH Academy... He will be formally registered at the Local Authority's Children's Support Service."*

This placement formula was considered in the case of *TB v Essex County Council [2013] UKUT 534 (AAC)*. AB, a young boy, had SEN related to behavioural problems that might have been associated with ADHD and autism. As AB faced difficulties in a mainstream school, his parents decided to withdraw him. They believed that an independent school, which catered for children with autistic spectrum disorders, would be more suitable for AB.

The LA proposed that AB attend a unit called GROW at WH Academy, which aimed to support pupils with behavioural issues and to facilitate their reintegration into mainstream schools. The LA argued against the placement in an independent school, owing to the cost. Under the proposed arrangement, AB would be formally registered with the LA's Children's Support Service (a pupil referral unit), while he would receive education in a separate portacabin located on WH Academy's premises.

The main question here was whether a "unit" within a school could be considered a separate school in its own right for the purposes of a placement request. It was determined that it could. Relevant factors that supported this decision included the presence of a management committee, a chain of command, and a designated teacher who worked specifically at GROW. As a result, AB's plan required the naming of two schools: the pupil referral unit and GROW at WH Academy.

In another case, the inclusion of the resource base as a placement in Section I was not feasible.

> *"PI be educated in "the Base" within the Central Primary School in the mornings in a class of eight with a teacher and two speech and language teaching assistants allocated to the class. In the afternoon he would go to mainstream classrooms of approximately thirty pupils."*

This SEP was discussed in the case of *JI and SP v Hertfordshire County Council [2020] UKUT 200 (AAC)*. "The Base" was part of Central Primary School and therefore could not be considered a separate school to be named in Section I of the EHCP. This created a dilemma regarding where the resource base should be named within the EHCP.

Section F was used to describe the SEP that was required by the child, including what would be provided by the Base, but the placement could not be named in it. Given that the child's placement in such a unit was vital to the suitability of the school, it is regrettable that such an important aspect could not be acknowledged or featured in the EHCP.

While in this case definitive answers may not be easily forthcoming, the LA and the family can engage in discussions to explore practical solutions.

One practical solution would be to name the school in Section I, with the resource base specified in brackets. This approach clarifies that the resource base is not a separate school, but also indicates that the child will be allocated a place at the resource base in terms of funding and provision. However, this solution is not perfect. Be mindful of a warning attributed to Judge Rowley in *NN v Cheshire East Council (SEN) [2021] UKUT 220 (AAC)*: any additions to Section I beyond the name and type of school may be considered an error of law.

Another option is to specify the type of school as, for example, "a mainstream school with an ASD resource base". By doing so, the role played by the resource base in determining the school's suitability for the child or young person is explicitly emphasised in the EHCP.

In such a scenario, it is essential that Section F contains a clear and detailed description of the SEP that the child or young person requires, which the resource base will provide. This ensures that the specific support and services offered by the resource base are well-documented and understood within the EHCP.

When Section I is left blank

Under Section 61(1) of the CFA 2014, an LA in England may arrange for any SEP to be made other than in a school or post-16 institution, or other than at a place where relevant early-years education is provided. Generally, this involves educating the child or young person at home.

The LA can only do this if it is satisfied that it would be inappropriate for the provision to be made in a school or post-16 institution. This scenario is commonly referred to as EOTAS.

If the provision is to be made outside a school or institution, the question becomes how it should be mentioned in the EHCP. Since "home" cannot be specified in Section I because it is not an institution attended by the child, the current practice is to leave Section I blank. This is because it is considered that in this situation the duty under Section 39(5) or Section 40(2) of the CFA 2014 simply does not arise. Therefore, Section I should be left blank, and the required provision is described in Section F.

Take a moment

Take a moment to reflect on the significance of the education sections in an EHCP.

How do these sections play a crucial role in shaping the education experience of a child or young person?

You can write down your thoughts and ideas or anything you consider important here.

Chapter 6:
Health sections (C and G)

Introduction

This chapter covers how health needs and provision are outlined in an EHCP. The plan should clearly state any health needs that are related to the child's or young person's SEN and that were found during the EHC needs assessment or any re-assessment.

Certain health needs directly affect a child's or young person's education, such as specific medical requirements – for example, medication or specialised equipment. Therapy provisions that are essential for the child to participate fully in educational activities are occasionally put in Section G, which may cause issues with their enforcement. It is preferable to place interventions that are vital for a child or young person to be able to access education in Section F. This chapter explores the distinction between Sections F and G, and emphasises the importance of putting things in the right place within the EHCP to gain effective support.

Section C: the child or young person's health needs that relate to their SEN

Here are the content guidelines for Section C, as they appear in the SEND COP 2015 (the table in Paragraph 9.69).

> - *"The EHC plan must specify any health needs identified through the EHC needs assessment which relate to the child or young person's SEN. Some health care needs, such as routine dental health needs, are unlikely to be related.*
> - *The Clinical Commissioning Group (CCG)* may also choose to specify other health care needs which are not related to the child or young person's SEN (for example, a long-term condition which might need management in a special educational setting)."*
>
> *According to the NHS website, Integrated Care Boards (ICBs) replaced CCGs in the NHS in England from 1 July 2022.

To qualify for an EHCP, a child or young person must have SEN, but they are not required to have health needs. Therefore, there is no need to provide information regarding all health needs – only those that are connected to SEN should be listed.

The data that should be included in this section will vary depending on individual circumstances and needs. By way of example, information about the regular administration of medication for conditions such as asthma or epilepsy during school hours should be included. Information should also be outlined about specific medical procedures that will affect the child's or young person's school life and with which professionals in a school or special educational setting need to be familiar, such as catheterisation or a feeding tube. The goal is to ensure that the child or young person receives optimal care and support throughout their education journey.

The SEND COP 2015 states that routine dental health needs are generally not considered to be related to SEN (Paragraph 9.69 of the SEND COP 2015). Yet dental health may sometimes have an impact on a child's or young person's participation in school. Although this distinction is made in the SEND COP 2015, there are instances in which children and young people with SEN may require the help of dental or healthcare professionals who are specifically trained to address their needs. If dental support is required for the child to engage fully in their education, these unique circumstances must be considered.

The Integrated Care Board (ICB), previously known as the Clinical Commissioning Group (CCG), may also choose to specify other healthcare needs that are not related directly to the child's or young person's SEN.

Section G: any health provision reasonably required due to the learning difficulties or disabilities that result in the child or young person having SEN

Here are the content guidelines for Section G, as they appear in the SEND COP 2015 (the table in Paragraph 9.69).

- *"Provision should be detailed and specific and should normally be quantified, for example, in terms of the type of support and who will provide it.*
- *It should be clear how the provision will support achievement of the outcomes, including the health needs to be met and the outcomes to be achieved through provision secured through a personal (health) budget.*
- *Clarity as to how advice and information gathered has informed the provision specified.*
- *Healthcare provision reasonably required may include specialist support and therapies, such as medical treatments and delivery of medications, occupational therapy and physiotherapy, a range of nursing support, specialist equipment, wheelchairs and continence supplies. It could include highly specialist services needed by only a small number of children, which are commissioned centrally by NHS England (for example, therapeutic provision for young offenders in the secure estate).*
- *The local authority and CCG may also choose to specify other health care provision reasonably required by the child or young person, which is not linked to their learning difficulties or disabilities, but which should sensibly be coordinated with other services in the plan.*

> ■ *See Paragraph 9.141 [of the SEND COP 2015] for details of duties*
> *on the health service to maintain the health care provision in the*
> *EHC plan."*

Section G is focused on healthcare provision, which is defined in Section 21(3) of the CFA 2014:

> *""Healthcare provision" means the provision of healthcare services as*
> *part of the comprehensive health service in England continued under*
> *section 1(1) of the National Health Service Act 2006."*

The support that the child or young person needs must be described in this section in detail and specifics. Check to see that the support needed is quantified as much as possible and confirm that the individuals who will be responsible for delivering this support are clearly indicated (use the "who, what, when and how long" writing formula). If your child is in or beyond Year 9 (ie, they are 13 years old or older), the healthcare support should also be tailored to help them to prepare for adulthood and to become more independent.

This section can only include the support that is "reasonably required" due to the learning difficulties and disabilities that result in the child or young person having SEN. What is reasonable varies according to each situation.

Before healthcare provision can be included, the responsible commissioning body must approve it, as stated in Regulation 12(2) of the SEND Regulations 2014. Once the healthcare provision is specified in this section, the relevant health commissioning body must arrange that specified provision for the child or young person, as outlined in Section 42(3) of the CFA 2014. See Paragraph 9.141 of the SEND COP 2015 for details of the duties of the health service to maintain the healthcare provision that is named in the EHCP.

Healthcare provision or SEP?

Certain healthcare services that contribute to a child's or young person's education or training are considered SEP and require specification in Section F of the plan. This is backed by Section 21(5) of the CFA 2014. We can use the following scenario to investigate how this works.

Robert, a ten-year-old boy, is diagnosed as autistic with several related conditions.

He has a language disorder that is associated with autism and is receiving support from a speech and language therapist, who has developed a programme of exercises for him.

Robert also has an avoidant and restrictive food intake disorder due to taste and texture hypersensitivities. This condition limits him to a small selection of preferred foods and requires specialised nutritional support. He is allowed to eat his lunch in a quiet place away from other children. He is working with a psychologist to address his food-related anxiety.

Robert has also been diagnosed with an auditory processing disorder. This condition affects his ability to process sounds, particularly in his left ear. There are also subtle issues with cochlear sound analysis in his right ear. Robert uses a personal FM system (an assistive listening device) to enhance his speech comprehension in noisy environments.

The help mentioned in this scenario comes from healthcare professionals. The health needs stem from Robert's SEN and/or the disability, so they must be included in the EHCP. The question is whether they should be classified as SEP or as healthcare support.

We can work through this scenario using the following approach (Table 5), which looks at each of the requirements and asks whether it educates or trains. The answer in each case will direct us towards the section(s) of the EHCP in which the information should be detailed.

Table 5: Evaluation of health requirements across EHCP sections

What is required?	Educates or trains?	EHCP section
Speech and language therapy	Yes, the programme is designed to improve communication and social skills.	Section B (needs) Section F (provision)
Quiet place for lunch	No, this relates to health needs, and it does not involve any training or education.	Section C (needs) Section G (provision)
Psychological help with food related anxiety	Yes, the goal is to equip Robert with the knowledge, skills, and tools to manage and overcome food-related anxiety and establish a healthier relationship with food.	Section B (needs) Section F (provision)
FM system	No, this relates to health needs, and it does not involve any training or education.	Section C (needs) Section G (provision)

Take a moment

Take a moment to reflect on what you have just read.

Consider the process that is used to assess and identify health needs for inclusion in the EHCP.

What considerations and factors might be involved in determining these needs?

Chapter 7:
Social care sections (D, H1 and H2)

Introduction

This chapter is focused on how social care needs and provision are described within an EHCP. The plan should highlight any social care needs that are reported during the EHC needs assessment and that are related to the child's or young person's SEN. It should also address needs that must be met for those under 18 under the Chronically Sick and Disabled Persons Act 1970 (CSDPA 1970). Additionally, the LA might choose to include other social care needs that are not directly linked to SEN or disability.

Note that social care falls under a different legislative framework, distinct from the CFA 2014. The EHC needs assessment does not extend to social care; its purpose is solely to evaluate care needs in sufficient detail for the LA to decide whether social care support is required. Therefore, it is necessary to follow a distinct process to identify and address social care needs. Guidance on navigating these procedures is provided below.

This chapter also explores the differentiation between Sections F and H, highlighting where it is important to distinguish SEP from social care provision.

Section D: the child or young person's social care needs that relate to their SEN or to a disability

Here are the content guidelines for Section D, as written in the SEND COP 2015 (the table in Paragraph 9.69).

■ *"The EHC plan must specify any social care needs identified through the EHC needs assessment which relate to the child or young person's SEN or which require provision for a child or young person under 18 under Section 2 of the Chronically Sick and Disabled Persons Act 1970.*

■ *The local authority may also choose to specify other social care needs which are not linked to the child or young person's SEN or to a disability. This could include reference to any child in need or child protection plan which a child may have relating to other family issues such as neglect. Such an approach could help the child and their parents manage the different plans and bring greater co-ordination of services. Inclusion must only be with the consent of the child and their parents."*

Section D must mention any social care needs that go along with the child's SEN or disability. The LA can also decide to specify other types of help. This might include a reference to any child in need or a child protection plan. Such information can only be included if both the child and their parents agree to it.

Often, when LAs ask social services for advice, the response they receive is that social services do not know the child or that the family does not want help. If you would like help, it is okay to question this answer. This is especially important in cases in which the young person is over 16 years old. As that young person moves towards adulthood, social services can offer support with things such as finding a place to live (eg, sheltered or supported housing). They can also help the young person to look for a job and to become more independent.

Consider whether a child or young person might have unaddressed social care needs. When families find themselves struggling with caregiving responsibilities, they might be eligible for various forms of support, such as respite care. If you explore the possibility of a social care assessment, you can gain information about the assistance that might be available.

If you need help from social services, the best thing to do is to ask for a full care assessment. This process should lead to the creation of a detailed care plan. The assessment type will vary based on the child's or young person's age.

For those under 18, the assessment is carried out under Section 17 of the Children Act 1989 and should adhere to the national guidance issued by the Secretary of State, which is published as *Working Together to Safeguard Children 2013*. Paragraph 10.18 of the SEND COP 2015 provides that "EHC needs assessments should be combined with social care assessments under Section 17 of the Children Act 1989 where appropriate".

For those over 18, assessments follow the adult social care procedures of the Care Act 2014.

Section H – introduction

Since Section H is divided into two parts, a brief introduction is needed.

According to Section 21(4) of the CFA 2014, social care provision is defined as follows:

> "'Social care provision' means the provision made by a local authority in the exercise of its social services functions."

The CFA 2014 distinguishes between children (typically up to age 16) and young people. In parallel, social care law is divided into two separate regimes: one for children under 18 and another for adults. This arrangement may raise some questions and highlights the need to understand both child and adult social care to navigate entitlements effectively. This book does not explore these systems in depth, but it is worthwhile to acknowledge this potential source of confusion.

Both Sections H1 and H2 impose obligations on the LA. However, the responsibility to provide the required support arises from social care legislation, not the CFA 2014.

Section H1: any social care provision that must be made for the child or young person as a result of Section 2 of the CSDPA 1970

Here are the content guidelines for Section H1, as they are written in the SEND COP 2015 (the table in Paragraph 9.69).

- *"Provision should be detailed and specific and should normally be quantified, for example, in terms of the type of support and who will provide it (including where this is to be secured through a social care direct payment).*

- *It should be clear how the provision will support achievement of the outcomes, including any provision secured through a Personal Budget. There should be clarity as to how advice and information gathered has informed the provision specified.*

- *Section H1 of the EHC plan must specify all services assessed as being needed for a disabled child or young person under 18, under Section 2 of the CSDPA. These services include:*

  - *practical assistance in the home;*

  - *provision or assistance in obtaining recreational and educational facilities at home and outside the home;*

  - *assistance in travelling to facilities;*

  - *adaptations to the home;*

  - *facilitating the taking of holidays;*

  - *provision of meals at home or elsewhere;*

  - *provision or assistance in obtaining a telephone and any special equipment necessary; and*

  - *non-residential short breaks (included in Section H1 on the basis that the child as well as his or her parent will benefit from the short break).*

- *This may include services to be provided for parent carers of disabled children, including following an assessment of their needs under sections 17ZD-17ZF of the Children Act 1989.*

> ■ See Paragraph 9.137 [of the SEND COP 2015] onwards for details of duties on local authorities to maintain the social care provision in the EHC plan."

As in other provision sections in the EHCP, support included in H1 should be detailed, specific and usually quantified – for example, in terms of the type of support and who will provide it (including in cases in which it is to be secured through a social care direct payment).

Section H2: any other social care provision reasonably required due to the learning difficulties or disabilities that result in the child or young person having SEN

Here are the content guidelines for Section H2, as they appear in the SEND COP 2015 (the table in Paragraph 9.69).

> ■ "Social care provision reasonably required may include provision identified through early help and children in need assessments and safeguarding assessments for children. Section H2 must only include services which are not provided under Section 2 of the CSDPA. For children and young people under 18, this includes residential short breaks and services provided to children arising from their SEN but unrelated to a disability. This should include any provision secured through a social care direct payment. See Chapter 10 for more information on children's social care assessments.
>
> ■ Social care provision reasonably required will include any adult social care provision to meet eligible needs for young people over 18 (set out in an adult care and support plan) under the Care Act 2014. See Chapter 8 for further detail on adult care and EHC plans.
>
> ■ The local authority may also choose to specify in Section H2 other social care provision reasonably required by the child or young person, which is not linked to their learning difficulties or disabilities. This will enable the local authority to include in the EHC plan social care provision such as child in need or child protection plans, or provision meeting eligible needs set out in an adult care plan where it is unrelated to the SEN but appropriate to include in the EHC plan.

> ■ See Paragraph 9.137 [of the SEND COP 2015] onwards for details of
> duties on local authorities to maintain the social care provision in the
> EHC plan."

Note that only relevant social care support that is considered
"reasonable" can be included in Section H2 – what is reasonable varies
according to the situation. This kind of support might come from
assessments done for early help and "children in need" assessments or
from safeguarding assessments for children.

The social care support in Section H2 might also include adult social care
provision for young people over 18 who have eligible needs, as set out in
a plan prepared under the Care Act 2014.

Social care provision or SEP?

Certain social care services that contribute to a child's or young person's
education or training are considered as SEP and therefore they must be
specified in Section F of the plan. This is backed by Section 21(5) of the
CFA 2014.

Let's consider the following scenario:

Dima, aged 13, is autistic and has a diagnosis of pathological demand
avoidance (PDA). He lives with his family, including three siblings,
and his parents are responsible for his care. His family observes that
he has to be reminded to do basic self-care tasks such as dressing
appropriately, maintaining oral hygiene, eating regularly, and going
to bed at a reasonable time. Without help, he struggles to take care
of himself. The family receives respite care in the form of a weekend
away for Dima every six months. Dima is actively seeking social
interaction opportunities and participates in local dance classes.
Because of his social anxiety, he requires help when travelling to
these classes. He is currently enrolled in a travel training course that is
aimed at fostering his independence.

The social care needs in this scenario stem from SEN and/or the disability, so they must be included in the EHCP. The next decision is whether the help needed should be classified as SEP or as social care support.

As with healthcare needs, one can work through this scenario by considering each of the child's or young person's requirements and asking whether it educates or trains (Table 6). The answer in each case will direct us towards the section(s) of the EHCP in which the information should be written.

Table 6: Evaluation of social care requirements across EHCP sections

What is required?	Educates or trains?	EHCP section
Respite care	No, this relates to social needs and it does not involve any training or education.	Section D (needs) Section H (provision)
Travel training	Yes, it is a training provision.	Section B (needs) Section F (provision)

Take a moment

As part of your reflections, you might want to consider the significance of the social care sections in an EHCP.

How do these sections contribute to the overall well-being and social development of the child or young person?

Chapter 8:
Other sections (A, E, J and K)

Introduction

The EHCP sections considered in this chapter are generally not open to appeal, but they are important for the plan's operation.

Section A outlines the child's or young person's aspirations and goals.

Section E covers various outcomes in education, health and care.

Section J details any personal budget that is agreed upon for EHCP provision and addresses direct payments.

Lastly, Section K catalogues the advice and information that has been collected during and after the EHC needs assessment.

Section A: the views, interests and aspirations of the child and their parents or the young person

Section A is of significant value as it allows the child or young person and their family to directly share their thoughts and perspectives in writing. This aspect sets this section apart from other parts of the plan.

Here are the content guidelines for Section A, as contained in the table in Paragraph 9.69 of the SEND COP 2015. The following could be included in Section A:

- *"Details about the child or young person's aspirations and goals for the future (but not details of outcomes to be achieved – see section above on outcomes for guidance). When agreeing the aspirations, consideration should be given to the child or young person's aspirations for paid employment, independent living and community participation.*

- *Details about play, health, schooling, independence, friendships, further education and future plans including employment (where practical).*
- *A summary of how to communicate with the child or young person and engage them in decision-making.*
- *The child or young person's history.*
- *If written in the first person, the plan should make clear whether the child or young person is being quoted directly, or if the views of parents or professionals are being represented."*

Think of Section A as a valuable space for your input.

Section 19 of the CFA 2014 mandates LAs to consider these views. While other parts of the plan may be subject to amendments based on professional advice, Section A should only be altered by parents or the young person. Essentially, it serves as a platform for them to articulate their views, interests and aspirations without unnecessary interference.

LAs usually offer templates for this section that provide a structured approach for those writing it. There is no legal obligation to follow these templates and Section A can be completed by including the information specified in Paragraph 9.96 of the SEND COP 2015. There is also no requirement by law to write anything at all in this section if you choose not to do so.

The templates guide parents and young people on what questions to answer and how to arrange their responses. Sometimes, this section is referred to as "All About Me". Some LAs offer a separate document in which parents can create a profile of the child.

Many of these templates incorporate visual elements such as colourful pictures and symbols, which brighten the overall presentation. Such formats provide a creative opportunity to showcase the child's journey. Some parents go above and beyond what is required and create almost miniature scrapbooks dedicated to their children's lives.

Both parents and children should share their perspectives, interests, and aspirations. Young people aged 16 and above should take the lead in completing this section – although input from parents is welcomed if desired or necessary.

It is important to acknowledge that the perspectives of parents and their children may differ. A child or young person with learning difficulties or a disability may have specific preferences regarding how they want to be described. It is necessary to be mindful about the language you use to characterise difficulties, as negative messaging about disability may have influenced your or their perception.

Have a conversation with your child about how they wish to be talked about. They might express a preference for identity-first language, such as being referred to as a "disabled person", rather than person-first (a "person with a disability"). Some neurodivergent individuals find person-first language offensive, as they view their neurological differences as an integral part of themselves that cannot be separated.

Here is an example of different language use:

- Neuro-negative expression: *"He suffers from autism spectrum disorder."*
- Neuro-affirmative expression: *"He is autistic and his development follows an autistic trajectory rather than the neurotypical developmental path."*

The words you choose have a powerful impact on how children view themselves and how others see them. You will often find terms such as "symptoms", "impairments" and "abnormalities" in reports, and they can make things sound pretty heavy. Such deficit-based language and thinking revolve around person's limitations or what they cannot do. However, you have the option to embrace strengths-based language when you describe your child, highlighting their qualities, resources and talents.

Consider the following example:

- Deficit-based language: *"She is a low-functioning child with autism who lacks cognitive flexibility and social skills."*
- Person-centred language: *"She currently has high support needs for mobility and requires assistance at social events. She has lower support needs when speaking up for herself (self-advocacy), with an expressed communication preference to be contacted via text or email."*

Choose your words carefully when you talk about a child who does not speak or use words. There is a difference between "non-verbal" and "non-speaking". Saying someone is "non-verbal" might imply that they lack both internal and external language, but that may not be true. Just because a child or young person does not speak does not mean they do not have their own way of understanding and expressing themselves.

Here is an example:

- Deficit-based language: *"She is non-verbal and faces challenges in expressing herself."*
- Person-centred language: *"She is non-speaking – she uses gestures, facial expressions and an electronic device to communicate."*

The invitation in the templates may suggest you write in the first person from the perspective of the child, but you can decide whether that is appropriate. You may instead choose to write as a parent – in which case, you express your own perspective rather than pretending to speak as your child.

Include your child's writings if they wish to express themselves. Their views are valued and legally must be taken into account; there is no need to worry that the LA will dismiss them. Parents are sometimes concerned that adding their children's views in the first person might make the plan seem too child-like, possibly taking away from the document's seriousness. The solution is to find a delicate balance that respects the child's voice while ensuring that the plan maintains a thoughtful and professional tone.

Bear in mind that the EHCP may remain in effect until the young person reaches 25 years of age. This prompts thoughtful consideration of both short-term and long-term goals. The extent of the support that is provided is directly influenced by the aspirations set in place.

In this context, it could be helpful to think about what you see as a good life for individuals with special needs. Society often uses financial criteria to judge what is meaningful. It is vital to look deeper, to consider how people might feel about their disabilities and to understand what causes those feelings.

Every person's life is important, no matter how much it costs to take care of them or how much they can do. Whether talking about big dreams or simple goals, prioritise and accommodate the person's preferences and experiences at the heart of the discussion.

In Section A, young people have a chance to practice speaking up and advocating for themselves. They can share what changes they need to be treated fairly. Learning to speak up is like opening a door to being true to oneself. By understanding what they need and asking for it, young people take an important step in being their real selves in all parts of their lives.

Section A of the EHCP also presents an opportunity to address matters that may not be immediately evident within the school setting. This section enables you to shed light on challenges that your child or young person may encounter at home, such as meltdowns or emotional episodes that happen because they feel compelled to mask their needs at school. Many reports that are written as evidence for the EHCP overlook or inadequately address these concerns and the school may struggle to grasp fully the extent of these difficulties or to offer the necessary support. Through Section A, it is possible to present a comprehensive picture that bridges gaps in understanding and covers all settings.

As you approach the writing of Section A, consider your audience. Depending on the child's stage of education, the main readers of this section might be their teachers or those at prospective schools during transfers. This section can be utilised to bring attention to specific issues.

Sometimes parents use Section A to convey their feelings regarding the process and the difficulties they have encountered within the system. In some cases, parents have submitted extensive accounts that span tens of pages. However, to ensure Section A's effectiveness, it is best avoid lengthy narratives. You can make a greater impact by keeping your content focused.

Section E: the outcomes sought for the child or the young person

As a reminder, only Section A is written by the parents and young people. The remaining sections (E, J, and K) are still drafted by the LA – although the family can make representations and suggest amendments.

Here are the content guidelines for Section E, as they appear in the SEND COP 2015 (the table in Paragraph 9.69). This is what Section E is required to include.

- *"A range of outcomes over varying timescales, covering education, health and care as appropriate but recognising that it is the education and training outcomes only that will help determine when a plan is ceased for young people aged over 18. Therefore, for young people aged over 17, the EHC plan should identify clearly which outcomes are education and training outcomes. See Paragraph 9.64 [of the SEND COP 2015] onwards for more detail on outcomes.*

- *A clear distinction between outcomes and provision. The provision should help the child or young person achieve an outcome, it is not an outcome in itself.*

- *Steps towards meeting the outcomes.*

- *The arrangements for monitoring progress, including review and transition review arrangements and the arrangements for setting and monitoring shorter term targets by the early-years provider, school, college or other education or training provider.*

- *Forward plans for key changes in a child or young person's life, such as changing schools, moving from children's to adult care and/or from paediatric services to adult health, or moving on from further education to adulthood.*

> ■ *For children and young people preparing for the transition to adulthood, the outcomes that will prepare them well for adulthood and are clearly linked to the achievement of the aspirations in Section A."*

The EHCP must clearly state the outcomes that are sought for the child or young person. Paragraph 9.66 of the SEND COP 2015 provides the following definition of an outcome:

> *"An outcome can be defined as the benefit or difference made to an individual as a result of an intervention… When an outcome is focused on education or training, it will describe what the expected benefit will be to the individual as a result of the educational or training intervention provided…"*

Section 19(d) of the CFA 2014 places great importance on outcomes and mandates LAs to support the development of children and young people and to make sure that the youngsters have the best opportunities to thrive. In essence, the law is aimed at ensuring that every child and young person is given the support and encouragement they need to achieve the very best for themselves, regardless of the challenges they face.

Outcomes differ from shorter-term targets. It is beneficial to add short-term plans with targets to the EHCP for consistent progress monitoring. The plan might incorporate scheduled meetings with parents throughout the year to assess progress. In exceptional cases, achievement of these shorter-term targets may prompt adjustments to individual outcomes before the annual review.

Section E is focused on the positive changes that a child or young person experiences when they receive help and support. However, achieving these outcomes does not happen in isolation. It may seem confusing that in the EHCP, Section E comes before all the provision sections. Ideally, it should come after them.

To better understand this point, consider first the child's or young person's needs as identified in Sections B, C and D. Then, explore the specific support or services that are required to address those needs, which can be found in Sections F, G and H. Once you have assessed needs and the corresponding provision, it is time to ask yourself: "What do we want to achieve through this support?" The answer is what is referred to as the outcome.

Sometimes, professionals and families brainstorm outcomes during the annual review, and they naturally lean towards the consideration of positive and comfortable goals. As a result, they tend to think of provision to meet these outcomes. This is not the right approach. Outcomes are important, but the provision should be aligned with meeting the child's or young person's needs in order to achieve the outcomes. So, try to think about things in this order: needs, provision and then outcomes.

When it comes to outcomes, the reason they play a vital role in the process is that if they are not regularly updated or if they have all been achieved without new ones added, the LA might view it as a sign that the EHCP is no longer necessary. They might propose to cease the plan as a result. Regularly updating outcomes ensures that, once a goal is achieved, there is a plan for the next one.

Outcomes are most effective when they are specific, measurable, achievable, realistic, and time-bound, which together is known as SMART. Take a closer look at each of these elements.

S – specific

The outcome should be clear and well-defined, with no ambiguity.

Let's consider an example of a specific outcome.

- Specific wording: *"By the end of the academic year, the pupil will be able to answer age-appropriate maths questions by identifying the required operation and confidently using various mathematical methods for calculations."*
- Non-specific wording: *"Improve maths skills."*

In the non-specific example, the outcome is vague and lacks clear direction. It simply states a desire to improve skills without providing any specific details on what level of improvement is expected. In contrast, the specific example sets a clear target.

M – measurable

There should be a way to assess or quantify the progress towards or achievement of the outcome.

Here is an example of a measurable outcome.

- Measurable wording: *"By the end of the term, the pupil will increase their spelling accuracy to at least 90% on weekly spelling tests."*
- Non-measurable wording: *"By the end of the term, the pupil will become better at spelling."*

In the measurable wording, a specific target is set for improvement, and a measurable criterion is provided for assessment. In contrast, the non-measurable wording lacks specificity and quantifiable criteria. It only states a general desire for improvement without any clear indication of what improvement means or how it will be measured.

A – achievable

"Achievable" and "realistic" elements of outcomes play important roles in goal-setting. However, there are no specific guidelines on how to distinguish them.

In simple terms, an achievable outcome is one that the child or young person has the capability and potential to reach. It considers the child's or young person's abilities and skills, and the target is made to be challenging yet within their reach, based on their current level of development and capacity for improvement.

By way of example, if the child or young person wants to improve their writing, an achievable outcome might be: *"By the end of the term, the pupil will improve their paragraph writing skills by organising their ideas into coherent sentences."*

R – realistic

On the other hand, a realistic outcome looks at whether the desired goal is feasible given the specific context and circumstances. It takes into account external factors such as time constraints, the available support, and the environment the child or young person is in. A realistic outcome sets a goal that is practical and can be accomplished given the resources and the child's or young person's limitations.

Let's consider an example of a realistic outcome.

- Realistic outcome: *"By the end of the term, the pupil will improve their reading fluency by one reading level, moving from a Level 3 to a Level 4 in the school's reading assessment."*
- Non-realistic outcome: *"By the end of the month, the pupil will become fluent in five different foreign languages."*

In the realistic outcome, the goal is set to be reached within a reasonable timeframe ("by the end of the term") and takes into account the pupil's current level (Level 3) to achieve an attainable improvement (moving to Level 4). In contrast, the non-realistic outcome is neither practical nor feasible.

T – time-bound

A timeframe should be set for the achievement of the outcome. This provides a sense of urgency and helps in the monitoring of progress towards the goal.

Here is an example of a time-bound or open-ended outcome:

- Time-bound outcome: *"By the end of the academic year, the pupil will demonstrate improved social interaction skills by initiating conversations with peers during structured activities at least three times per week."*
- Open-ended outcome: *"The pupil will continuously work on improving their fine motor skills to better manipulate small objects and hold a pencil with a more controlled grip."*

In the time-bound outcome, there is a specific deadline for the child or young person to show progress in social interaction skills. In contrast, the open-ended outcome highlights that the child's or young person's fine motor skill development is an ongoing process with no specific timeframe or deadline.

Outcomes are typically tied to the completion of a particular phase or stage in education. By way of example, an outcome might be set to be achieved by the end of the current Key Stage in school or by the time the child turns 11 (transition to secondary school) or 16 years old (end of compulsory schooling). This concept aligns with the guidance in Paragraph 9.69 of the SEND COP 2015, which highlights that outcomes should act as forward plans for important changes in a child's or young person's life, so that the outcome can help them to progress smoothly to the next stage.

Section J: personal budget (including arrangements for direct payments)

Here are the content guidelines for Section J, as they are written in the SEND COP 2015 (the table in Paragraph 9.69).

- *"This section should provide detailed information on any personal budget that will be used to secure provision in the EHC plan.*
- *It should set out the arrangements in relation to direct payments as required by education, health and social care regulations.*
- *The special educational needs and outcomes that are to be met by any direct payment must be specified."*

In general, the LA provides funds to the school or college for the education support that the child or young person needs and arranges external therapies that the EHCP specifies. If parents or the young person themselves are overseeing the provision, the LA must assess the potential for a personal budget. This can be requested either when the LA sends a draft EHCP after the EHC needs assessment or during a review of an existing plan. To be clear, a personal budget can be obtained only for someone who has an EHCP.

The LA may decline to allocate a personal budget in cases in which it pays a consolidated amount for SEP – which includes the provision needed for the child or young person – through arrangements with third parties. By way of example, this could be a contract with the NHS that covers speech and language or occupational therapy. A personal budget may not be appropriate if the notional amount that is allocated to the specified provision cannot be separated or disaggregated from the total sum that is paid through the contract, owing to potential adverse impacts on other services for children or young people with EHCPs, or because such separation would be an inefficient use of the LA's resources.

To illustrate, consider a scenario in which an LA arranges occupational therapy for individuals separately. In this case, the cost of the therapy – say £2,200 per year – can be determined easily. However, if the LA arranges to provide therapy on a group or block basis, it is hard to identify and disaggregate the exact amount that is paid for each individual. In such circumstances, the LA may not be obliged to grant a personal budget.

Under certain conditions, the LA can offer direct payments to you, the young person, or a nominated individual who must meet certain requirements, as part of a personal budget so that you or they can organise the provision required (Section 49(3)(d) of the CFA 2014).

There is no automatic entitlement to direct payments. However, if a request for direct payments is made, the LA must consider it. If the request is denied, this decision can be contested through a judicial review.

One key limitation to remember about direct payments is that for services that are provided within a school, post-16 institution, or premises where relevant early-years education is offered, you need to obtain written consent from the headteacher, principal, or equivalent authority, or the provider of the relevant early-years education.

Such consent may be withheld if, for example, the setting lacks premises suitable for service provision. Other factors, such as the requirement for an up-to-date Disclosure and Barring Service (DBS) check, may also be applicable. It is wise to examine these requirements in advance and to explore potential solutions for any issues that may arise.

Section K: advice and information

Here are the content guidelines for Section K, as they appear in the SEND COP 2015 (the table in Paragraph 9.69).

- *"The advice and information gathered during the EHC needs assessment must be set out in appendices to the EHC plan. There should be a list of this advice and information."*

Section K is the final part of the EHCP. It outlines the reports that have been accepted and used by the LA to write the plan. Section K must be completed and should be included in every version of the plan. The list within Section K should contain details of the advice providers, including their names, specialist occupations, and the dates when the advice was given.

All the advice and information collected should be attached as appendices. The collection should include any private reports submitted by parents as part of their evidence. In some cases, the LA may argue against including private reports in Section K on the basis that it has not used the report's content in the EHCP. You can ask the LA to explain its reasons for such decisions and seek the inclusion of these reports. Be mindful that if any advice is not included in Section K, it may mean that its content is not reflected in other sections of the EHCP, including in the education sections (B, F, and I).

Take a moment

Take a moment to collect your thoughts and ideas, and write down anything that comes to mind.

You may like to reflect on the significance of Sections A, E, J, and K in an EHCP.

Chapter 9:
Putting it all together and keeping it relevant

This book has covered a lot of detail regarding the content of an EHCP. I hope it will be of great help assessing drafts written by the LA, but no one can be expected to keep all the points straight and to apply everything flawlessly to their specific situation at the first attempt.

The development of the EHCP will likely be a multi-step process, in which information is checked and rechecked, moved between sections, added to (or deleted) and reworded. Although this may be frustrating, it is to be expected and is part of the process.

EHCP checklist

The table below contains a checklist that consolidates the key points and that you can use as a handy reference tool.

Table 7: EHCP checklist

Content reference	Key points
Expert reports	To get started, take a close look at the evidence about the child's or young person's learning difficulties or disabilities (Chapter 3 will help you here).
	You can make it more organised by using a highlighter to emphasise important details or by creating a table.
	Repeat this process for SEP but use a different colour for highlights or add it to your table to match the needs.
	If there are health and social care needs and provision involved, be sure to mark those too.

Section A	Make sure the views, interests and aspirations of the child or young person are included, as well as those of their parents.
	Double-check that these aspirations are ambitious enough to align with the level of support required.
	The contents of this section are covered on pp.127-132.
Section B	Check that all SEN mentioned in the expert reports are listed under the appropriate category.
	The contents of this section are covered on pp.82-87.
	Did you try the 'Picture This' exercise that is described on pp.79-81?
	Did you make any notes on Chapter 5? Look at those too.
Section C	If any healthcare needs relate to SEN or a disability, check that they are recorded here.
	The contents of this section are covered on pp.113-115.
Section D	If there are any social care needs that relate to SEN or a disability, check that they are recorded here.
	The contents of this section are covered on pp.119-121.
Section E	Start by looking through the reports to see if they identify any outcomes.
	Make sure that outcomes are set for all the different areas of need and that they match the structure and content of Section B.

	Remember to be SMART!
	Check that arrangements to monitor progress are included here.
	The contents of this section are covered on pp.132-137.
Section F	Examine the SEP descriptions to ensure specificity, clarity on who is responsible, and alignment with SEN in Section B and achievable outcomes in Section E.
	If any aspect is unclear, refer to the reports or seek clarification from professionals.
	Be on the alert for "weasel words" (see Table 4)!
	If there is a need for future updates from professionals, check that the monitoring requirements have been documented in this section.
	The contents of this section are covered on pp.88-105.
	Did you try the 'Picture This' exercise that is described on pp.79-81?
	Did you make any notes on Chapter 5? Look at those too.
Section G	Check that all SEP is located correctly in Section F and not misplaced in Section G or elsewhere (exercise in Table 5 can help you to decide).
	Also, confirm the inclusion of any necessary healthcare provision.
	The contents of this section are covered on pp.115-116.

Section H1 Section H2	Check that all SEP is located correctly in Section F and not misplaced in Section H or elsewhere (exercise in Table 6 can help you to decide). Confirm the inclusion of any necessary social care provision. The contents of these sections are covered on pp.122-124.
Section I	Confirm that, at an absolute minimum, Section I of the final EHCP describes the type of placement. If agreed upon, the particular school should be named. In the case of EOTAS, this section should be blank. The contents of this section are covered on pp.105-112. Did you try the 'Picture This' exercise that is described on pp.79-81? Did you make any notes on Chapter 5? Look at those too.
Section J	If a personal budget has been agreed, check that the contents accurately reflect it. The contents of this section are covered on pp.137-138.
Section K	Verify that all reports and evidence have been included in this list. The contents of this section are covered on p.139.

Reviewing and monitoring the EHCP

The EHCP is a powerful tool that lays out the support that children and young people need to thrive in their academic life, social connections, and emotional well-being. Writing it is just the beginning of its impact. The EHCP is not a final destination and it is not set in stone. It is a living document that can be adapted to meet the child's or young person's evolving needs. As their story unfolds, be prepared to rewrite, revise and reimagine.

Securing an EHCP is a challenging struggle for many parents. Once obtained, many of them are suspicious about any attempts to modify it as there is a fear that the LA might seek to dilute its provisions. Being vigilant is undoubtedly wise, yet it is equally important to keep an open mind. Not all changes are inherently negative and the adjustments may be beneficial. The plan should be a fluid document that changes along with the child's unique needs as they grow.

To ensure this happens, LAs are required to look over EHCPs every year in a process called the "annual review". They have the power to amend the EHCP if there are changes in the child's or young person's situation or needs.

The information presented below gives a brief overview of the main points you need to know about the review process. Note that it is not intended to provide comprehensive coverage, as these topics lie outside the central subject matter of this book. This part is included for your quick reference; the signposting in 'Further reading' (see pp.147-148) below shows where further information can be found.

Annual review

The LA is required to conduct a review of an EHCP at least once every 12 months (Section 44(1) of the CFA 2014). However, the SEND COP 2015 recommends that these reviews should occur more frequently for children under the age of five – ideally every three to six months (Paragraph 9.178 of the SEND COP 2015). LAs can initiate an annual review ahead of schedule and a school or a parent/young person can request an early or emergency review.

Annual reviews provide good opportunities for parents and young people to seek up-to-date information and reports from professionals on changes that are required to descriptions of SEN and/or SEP in the EHCP.

The annual review is not just a meeting to discuss the EHCP. It is a process that encompasses all the steps the LA must take to evaluate thoroughly the situation and it concludes when the LA informs the parent or young person of its decision after it has received the report from the review meeting. The LA has three possible courses of action: to maintain the plan without changes, to change it, or to cease to maintain the plan.

The LA must confirm its decision in writing; otherwise, it obstructs a parent's or young person's right to appeal. The parent or young person can appeal only when they receive a written notice of this decision. If the LA fails to send this notification, reach out to the LA to request that the review be completed.

Monitoring progress

According to Section 44 of the CFA 2014, the LA must regularly check how well a child or young person is doing in achieving the goals set out in their EHCP. This generally happens during the annual review. Arrangements for tracking progress are written in Section E of the plan.

The SEP that is in place for the child or young person is there to ensure that they make good progress. In cases in which this is not evident, question whether all relevant SEN are accurately listed in Section B, and whether the level of SEP in Section F is correct. Sometimes, it might even be worth thinking about changing the school placement in Section I.

These considerations may lead to questions about whether or not the contents of the EHCP are still right for the child or young person. If you think the EHCP is not working, first take some time to read carefully what it actually says. Sometimes, the plan might include everything the child or young person needs, but it is not being properly followed. In such cases, you can take steps to ensure the plan is followed.

However, this depends on whether the plan is specific enough. Just as a chocolate teapot would be impractical for making tea, a vague or unclear plan might not serve its intended purpose. If the EHCP needs clarification, use the annual review to make it more precise.

If your child is under 16, you have the right to be actively involved in this process and to advocate for what is best for your child's education and well-being. Legal rights granted by the CFA 2014 are transferred from parents to young people around the age of 16 (for additional discussion see pp.70-73). From this point onwards, young people are invited to navigate matters related to EHCPs and arrangements for their education.

When someone reaches 18, they do not have to stay in school or training if they do not want to. Reaching adulthood is a crucial moment at which young people should speak up about what they need and want. This stage marks a critical juncture for fostering self-advocacy. Encouraging the young person to articulate their needs and aspirations empowers them to participate actively in shaping their education and transition plans.

For individuals over 18 who have EHCPs, Section 44(5) of the CFA 2014 provides specific guidelines for the annual review process. In order to discontinue the plan, the LA has to evaluate whether the education or training outcomes outlined in the plan have been achieved. If it becomes apparent that this is not the case, this information can serve as crucial support for the young person if they seek different or additional SEP. They can assert that this extra help is needed to reach important goals in order for them to move on to the next part of their life, such as getting a job, living on their own, or going to college. They might also need to be clear that they want the outcomes to be made more challenging if the ones they have are not big enough for their aspirations.

Further reading

For further in-depth information on annual reviews, you can refer to the comprehensive checklist prepared by IPSEA, which can be found on their website. In addition, you can contact IPSEA directly for advice and support via their helpline.

SOS!SEN's website has a wealth of resources. This includes a list of FAQs and myths about annual reviews, as well as access to a recorded webinar that offers useful insights. SOS!SEN also has a helpline and operates walk-in centres where you can meet its volunteers in person.

Special Needs Jungle offers a downloadable flowchart to help you navigate the annual review process.

You can find the website links to these charities in the "online resources" section at the end of this book.

Take a moment

Take a moment to write down your reflections.

Consider the role of collaboration between parents, educators, healthcare professionals, and social care providers in the review and monitoring process.

How might effective teamwork enhance the accuracy and relevance of the EHCP?

Final words

As I wrap up this guide, I cannot help but think about the stories that are yet to unfold for your children and for those young people who are finding their voice in self-advocacy. I like to imagine these tales as filled with achievements, personal growth, and the successful pursuit of happiness that will shape their unique narratives. The EHCP is not just paperwork – it is a key that can unlock the doors to education, remove barriers, and ultimately help children and young people to thrive within their studies.

I want to stress the importance of timely intervention. The longer a child goes without the support they need, the harder it becomes to bridge the gaps between what they are learning and what they could learn with the right help. Throughout this book, my sincere hope has been to provide you with the knowledge and tools necessary to write an EHCP that is not only comprehensive but actionable. This plan should be a beacon of opportunity and a roadmap tailored to the child's unique education journey. Their story is just beginning, and I wish wholeheartedly that it will be a happy and fulfilling one. If you are a young person continuing this journey, I hope you can make big improvements using what you have learned here. Please remember it is never too late to make positive changes in your life.

In closing, think back to the analogy that was used at the beginning of the book, which compared a poorly written EHCP to a chocolate teapot. Now you can imagine an improved version with this whimsical illustration. May your plan be strong, effective, and perfectly suited to meet needs.

Case law references

AB v North Somerset [2010] UKUT 8 (AAC)

AJ v LB Croydon [2020] UKUT 246 (AAC)

B-M and B-M v Oxfordshire CC (SEN) [2018] UKUT 35 (AAC)

DC and DC v Hertfordshire CC [2016] UKUT 379 (AAC)

DM v Cornwall County Council [2022] UKUT 230 (AAC)

Dudley MBC v Shurvinton [2012] EWCA Civ 346

E v Rotherham MBC [2002] ELR 266, [2001] EWHC Admin 432

EAM v East Sussex CC [2022] UKUT 193 (AAC)

East Sussex CC v TW [2016] UKUT 528 (AAC)

EC v North East Lincolnshire LA [205] UKUT 0648 (AAC)

H v Leicestershire [2000] ELR 471

IPSEA v Secretary of State (2003) EWCA Civ 07 (2003) ELR 86

JI and SP v Hertfordshire County Council [2020] UKUT 200 (AAC)

L v Clarke and Somerset [1998] ELR 129

London Borough of Redbridge v HO (SEN) [2020] UKUT 323 (AAC)

NN v Cheshire East Council (SEN) [2021] UKUT 220 (AAC)

R v Wandsworth ex parte M [1998] ELR 424

S v Special Educational Needs Tribunal [2005] EWHC 196 (Admin)

SG v Denbighshire CC [2018] UKUT 369 (AAC)

SB v Herefordshire County Council [2018] UKUT 141 (AAC)

TB v Essex County Council [2013] UKUT 534 (AAC)

Worcestershire County Council v SE [2020] UKUT 217 (AAC)

Online resources

bailii.org is the website of the British and Irish Legal Information Institute (BAILII). It is an online resource that offers free access to a vast collection of legal judgments, decisions, and legislation from the United Kingdom. It serves as a valuable platform for legal professionals, academics, students and the public to retrieve legal documents. This is a good resource through which to access tribunal judgements.

councilfordisabledchildren.org.uk is the official website of the Council for Disabled Children, which is an integral part of the National Children's Bureau family. Positioned as the umbrella organisation for the disabled children's sector, it brings together more than 300 voluntary and community organisations and an active network of practitioners across education, health, and social care. The website is a thorough resource that offers comprehensive information and support that is dedicated to children with SEN and disabilities.

gov.uk is the official website of the United Kingdom government. It is a central platform where you can find a wide range of government services and information. This is the place to find resources such as the SEND COP 2015, the SEND and Alternative Provision Improvement Plan, and school census.

ipsea.org.uk is the website of IPSEA, which is a prominent charity that offers free legal advice, resources and support to parents and carers of children with SEN and disabilities. It provides expert guidance on law, EHCPs, school placements and more.

legislation.gov.uk is a comprehensive resource that provides access to the official repository of the legislative acts in the United Kingdom. The CFA 2014 and various other Acts and regulations are here.

matrixlaw.co.uk and **landmarkchambers.co.uk** are websites where you can access the most recent edition of the *Noddy No-Nonsense Guide to SEN Law*. This guide consolidates important legal provisions, government guidelines and case law. It is a free public resource that is designed to assist anyone who deals with SEN law in England, including judges, legal and education professionals, LAs and parents.

mind.org.uk is the website of Mind, a reputable mental health charity based in the United Kingdom. Mind is known for its extensive resources, support and advocacy for individuals experiencing mental health challenges. Its website contains a wealth of information related to various aspects of mental health, including advice on seeking help, explanations of different mental health conditions, and strategies for maintaining good mental well-being. Additionally, Mind offers resources for those who want to support others who may be struggling with their mental health.

NHS.uk is the official website of the NHS in the United Kingdom. It is as a comprehensive resource that provides information and advice on a wide range of health-related topics.

sossen.org.uk is the website of SOS!SEN, an independent charity based in the United Kingdom that offers information, advice and support to parents and carers of children with SEN and disabilities. It provides expertise in navigating the complexities of the education system and helps families to access the appropriate support and resources for their children's unique needs.

specialneedsjungle.com is an informative website that provides resources, support and advocacy for parents and carers of children with SEN and disabilities. It offers a wealth of articles, guides and expert insights on topics related to special needs education, healthcare and social care. Special Needs Jungle provides a valuable platform for families who seek information, advice and practical tips to navigate the complex landscape of special education in the United Kingdom.